Between the Rivers:
The History of Ancient Mesopotamia
Part II: The Great City-States

Professor Alexis Q. Castor

THE TEACH

D1457264

PUBLISHED BY:

THE TEACHING COMPANY
4151 Lafayette Center Drive, Suite 100
Chantilly, Virginia 20151-1232
1-800-TEACH-12
Fax—703-378-3819
www.teach12.com

ISBN 1-59803-261-5

Alexis Q. Castor, Ph.D.

Assistant Professor of Classics,
Franklin & Marshall College

Alexis Q. Castor received her M.A. and Ph.D. in Classical and Near Eastern Archaeology from Bryn Mawr College. She received her B.A. in history from George Mason University and completed graduate courses in Greek, Roman, and Near Eastern History at The George Washington University.

Dr. Castor has taught at The George Washington University and has been a research associate at the Center for Advanced Study in the Visual Arts at the National Gallery of Art. Since 2000, she has taught ancient history, archaeology, and Greek at Franklin & Marshall College. In 2004, she team-taught "Between the Rivers," with Hilary Gopnik, Ph.D. In addition to survey courses of Greek and Roman history and archaeology, she has taught upper-level courses on Alexander the Great, the Hellenistic Near East, and the ancient house. She has been named Most Influential Professor by the senior class twice.

Dr. Castor's research interests are in the area of social history in the Greek world, specifically, the use of luxury goods to display status. In addition, she is interested in interconnections among Greece, the Black Sea, and Asia Minor.

Table of Contents
Between the Rivers:
The History of Ancient Mesopotamia
Part II: The Great City-States

Between the Rivers:
The History of Ancient Mesopotamia

Scope:

Six thousand years ago, in the land bordered by the Tigris and Euphrates Rivers, the first cities arose, ruled by kings who created complex bureaucracies that fostered the invention of writing and other technological advances. The Greeks coined the term *Mesopotamia*, "the land between the rivers," for this region, a name that the Romans later applied when they conquered the territory. In this course, we will explore Mesopotamian societies from the Neolithic era (c. 9,000 B.C.) to the defeat of the great Persian Empire at Gaugamela by Alexander the Great (331 B.C.). Our study will take us from the world of international diplomacy with powerful neighbors in Egypt, Syria, and Anatolia to the mundane issues of daily life, such as providing food for the family, curing disease, and settling legal disputes. We will examine archaeological discoveries, historical documents, and literary texts to explore how these lands between the rivers created a civilization that has contributed to the development of our own. A recurring theme of the course will be the creation of an urban lifestyle, which becomes increasingly sophisticated and complex as cultures expand.

This introduction to the history and culture of Mesopotamia is divided into three parts. We will begin by looking at the region in which we see the development of agriculture, settlements, and the rise of cities. What do these early cities look like? What can we say about the people who lived in them? How were they organized and in what professions did the populace engage? Temples were the earliest public architecture and required thousands of laborers to erect the structures; the organization of this labor force results in an early form of bureaucracy. Because much of the evidence for this era derives from archaeological remains, we will explore the methods used to reconstruct history from artifacts ranging from broken pieces of pottery to city walls.

In the second part of the course, we will study how the early city-states grew in size and complexity. Rulers promoted building projects, encouraged trade, and protected their people from harm. The ideal ruler was hailed as the shepherd of his people who had the favor of the gods. Literature and art celebrate the king in these roles, and we see energetic leaders digging irrigation canals and dedicating temples to the gods. During this era, we will meet historical figures, such as Hammurabi, the king of Babylon in the 18th century B.C. Hammurabi is most famous for his law code, in which the ruler legislates a wide range of punishments for theft, property disputes, and familial quarrels. Sentences are levied based on one's social standing; these laws reveal a strictly hierarchical society in which the wealthy man pays fines, while the poor man suffers more extreme physical punishment.

International contacts with other areas of the Near East flourish at this time. We will examine diplomatic correspondence between the great cities in Mesopotamia and the powerful states of Egypt and Syria, as well as the influence visible in the art and architecture of the era. Society grew ever more complex and cultured. Developments in such fields as medicine and astronomy reveal the Mesopotamian interest in understanding and ordering the world.

The last section of the course will explore the rise of empires, specifically, the great Assyrian and Persian empires. A strongly militaristic society, the Assyrians dominated much of the Near East and effected enormous cultural changes for the peoples of this region through their practice of mass transfers of population. Enormous palaces displayed images of their kings engaged in lion hunts and at the head of the mighty Assyrian army, reinforcing the strength of the state. Such a disciplined society required the smooth transfer of power from ruler to ruler to oversee the complicated bureaucracy necessary to control an empire of such great size. When palace intrigues weakened the throne, the neighboring Medes and Persians quickly seized power and established themselves at the head of the empire.

The interaction between the East and the West is the focus of the last six lectures of the course. During this time, the small and distant country of Greece was able to fend off two invasions led by the Persian king Darius and his son Xerxes in the early 5th century B.C. Although these defeats had little impact on the Persian Empire, which flourished for another century and a half, they were significant for the Greeks. The Greek historian Herodotus recorded these events from the side of the victors, and his account had enormous influence on the way that later generations of scholars understood the peoples of Mesopotamia. Despite the image that Herodotus and other Greek authors drew of a weak and corrupt Persian state, it remained a wealthy and vital empire that fell only as a result of the military brilliance of Alexander the Great. Alexander's victory allowed him to rule briefly at the head of the largest empire then known, reaching from Greece to western India, but after his death in Babylon in 323 B.C., no single ruler was able to control these lands again. Many of the great cities of Mesopotamia were abandoned, known only as legends until archaeologists uncovered them 2,000 years later.

Lecture Thirteen
The Royal Cemetery at Ur

Scope:

In this lecture, we will continue to see the power of the ruler displayed to his subjects, in this case, on the occasion of his burial. As noted in Lecture Three, a spectacular and widely publicized archaeological discovery was the Royal Cemetery at Ur, excavated in the late 1920s by Sir Leonard Woolley. This extensive burial ground included grave gifts of gold, silver, imported alabaster, lapis lazuli, and carnelian. Some graves were constructed with multiple chambers. These larger burials contained a wealth of exotic goods to comfort the dead in the afterlife: musical instruments, chariots, jewelry, and even ritually slaughtered human attendants. Although many questions concerning the meaning of these extraordinary tombs remain unanswered, they reveal much about the funerary customs for members of the political, religious, or social elite.

Outline

I. Ur had been known for many years because of the large ziggurat mound that dominated the site. Visitors to the region had described the site in the 17th century A.D., and initial excavations began in the mid-19th century.

    A. After World War I, Sir Leonard Woolley led a joint expedition at Ur, sponsored by the British Museum and the University of Pennsylvania.

    B. Woolley cleared the ziggurat and explored the temple of Nanna, patron deity of Ur, including portions of the temple that had been restored and expanded by the Babylonian king Nebuchadnezzar.

    C. In the sixth year of excavation, the team began to uncover a large group of graves that lay below the foundation of these later structures.

        1. Almost 2,000 graves were discovered, but 16 of these were so spectacular that newspapers reported their excavation in detail.

2. These "royal graves," as they were quickly termed, contained lavish quantities of gold, silver, and semiprecious stones, but the most surprising feature of the burials was the suggestion that they provided evidence of human sacrifice.

II. The Standard of Ur, now housed in the British Museum, is a wooden box, about a foot long, covered with lapis lazuli, white shell, and red limestone. It has three rows of scenes on both long sides.

A. The longest side shows a battle. In the top center, a large figure, probably a ruler, faces a row of captives; behind the ruler are arrayed soldiers carrying spears, and behind them is a chariot with donkeys.

B. On the opposite side, we move from the battle to a banquet.

1. Again, on the top is the largest figure; here, the king is seated, wearing a fleecy skirt, holding a cup, and facing a row of seated males who wear plain skirts with fringe and also hold cups. Behind them is a standing male who holds a lyre with a ram head protome.

2. The lower two registers show men leading animals and bringing food, recalling the Uruk Vase we discussed earlier.

3. The distinctions in dress and animal species reveal that these men and animals come from different regions in Mesopotamia. This is the first time that we see specificity in dress indicating a regional style, which will become a typical feature of later art.

C. The Standard of Ur was probably attached to a pole and carried; it would be an effective symbol of kingship, illustrating two of the ruler's most important functions.

III. Musical instruments also figure among the unusual artifacts from Ur. Examples of these are in the Iraq Museum, the British Museum, and the University of Pennsylvania Museum.

A. Lyres were large instruments, about 4 to 5 feet high, held with straps around the shoulders.

1. The lyres are wooden with metal and stone overlay. In his excavations, Woolley preserved and consolidated

these artifacts by pouring plaster over them so that the pieces would cling together.

2. The lyres are decorated with sculptures of animal heads, particularly bulls, and decorative inlays. The bulls are sheathed in gold on the head and horns, with lapis used for tufts of hair, at the tips of the horns, and to create a long, curly beard.

3. The front of one lyre was decorated with a panel of carved shell showing animals and mythical creatures. At the top, a hero clasps two bulls with human heads; the meaning of this image is unclear, but it may refer to some story about the underworld.

4. The three lower registers show animals involved in a funeral banquet and a small animal band. A donkey is playing a lyre just like the instrument we are describing; a bear stands in front of the lyre; and a fox is seated before it.

5. The bottom row represents a mythical half-human, half-scorpion figure and a gazelle standing upright and holding beakers.

B. Stringed instruments of different sizes are common at Ur and show that music was an important part of the funeral ritual.

IV. Most Mesopotamian graves were simple pits dug into the ground; the royal graves, however, consisted of larger chambers made of brick or stone. This more elaborate construction would require additional labor, which we may interpret as a sign of the ruler's prestige.

A. The graves are vaulted, rectangular chambers situated at the bottom of a ramp. Inside the graves, Woolley found bodies surrounded by many grave goods and, in some graves, a sled that presumably brought the corpses inside.

B. Numerous other bodies were found in the chambers or, more often, lying outside of them; these were probably attendants.

C. Several royal tombs were built next to each other; presumably, the first tomb was built and successors were then buried nearby.

D. Within these 16 royal graves, there is great variation in the size of the tombs and the number of bodies of both sexes buried in them.

E. The grave of one male is a chamber built of stone and brick, about 12 by 6 feet. This grave was robbed in antiquity, but outside it, what Woolley termed the "death pit" was intact.

    1. The bodies of 60 individuals, mostly women, were found on the ramp. Six soldiers, who carried spears and wore helmets, were outside the chamber, as were six oxen, drawing two wagons, and a groom and a driver.

    2. The women were lined up in a row along a wall; they were very richly adorned and likely carried the lyres found nearby.

F. Very near the death pit was the grave of a woman named Pu-Abi; her name was inscribed on a cylinder seal with the title *nin*, which means "queen." She was about 40 and buried in a chamber tomb of about 12 by 6 feet.

    1. Pu-Abi's burial costume was quite elaborate. She wore a headdress made of strips of sheet gold woven together to create a cap of shimmering leaves and flowers, a comb worn at the back of her head, and a gold wreath.

    2. In addition, this queen wore a cape made of gold, silver, lapis, carnelian, and agate beads; long strings of these colorful beads hung from her shoulders to her waist.

    3. Beneath the cape was a belt of horizontal beads, mostly lapis with alternating rows of gold and carnelian, as well as a rich array of other jewelry.

    4. Three other bodies were found in Pu-Abi's chamber tomb, including a male and a female who were probably attendants.

    5. Other goods buried with the queen included numerous gold and silver cups, stone bowls, furniture inlays, and cosmetic boxes.

V. Woolley identified a death pit associated with Pu-Abi's burial, but subsequent reexamination questioned that conclusion.

A. On the ramp leading to the burial chamber of Pu-Abi were the bodies of several attendants, both male and female. Ten women were placed in two rows facing one another, holding harps and lyres.

B. These women wore costumes similar to that of Pu-Abi but much less elaborate. The bodies of the men in this death pit were also adorned with jewelry, and each carried a dagger and a whetstone.

C. In addition to the humans found in the grave, the bones of two oxen were identified.

VI. These two graves offer definite evidence for human sacrifice accompanying the burial of a man and a woman of high status, probably a ruler and his wife. The amount of gold and other expensive goods buried in the chambers gives us an idea of the objects royals used and suggests that they possessed enormous wealth.

A. These burials also let us imagine early funeral rituals. We can't know if the elaborate costume of Pu-Abi was something she wore only for special occasions, but we can see how her dress would set her apart from others who were dressed more simply.

B. The musical instruments may have been used to play a dirge or hymn, followed by death for the musicians. Woolley suggested that they may have drunk poison. This would have been the ultimate symbol of a ruler's power.

C. The ritual suicide could well have been voluntary. The attendants may have desired to keep working for their rulers in the afterlife, or perhaps, the rulers needed servants in the afterlife and compelled their attendants to join them in death.

VII. Scholars continue to puzzle over the significance of these tombs, especially given that they remain unique discoveries.

A. Only one of the artifacts, a gold vessel, is inscribed with the name of a known ruler, Meskalamdug.

B. The other inscribed artifacts, such as the seal with Pu-Abi's name, were found in the area of the grave but not in the chamber with the main tomb occupant.

C. The biggest puzzle revolves around the practice of ritual murder or suicide. Why was this act considered necessary at this time?

1. There are no known comparable examples of ritual murder accompanying a burial in Mesopotamia at this time.

2. The story of the death of Gilgamesh records, however, that he was buried with the female members of his family and courtiers.
3. Outside of Mesopotamia, there are examples of ritual murder in other cultures.

VIII. The wealth of the graves at the Royal Cemetery is overwhelming; add to that the evidence for mass suicide upon the death of the ruler, and we get a real sense of the power of a king and queen.

Essential Reading:

Richard Zettler and Lee Horne, eds., *Treasures from the Royal Tombs at Ur.*

Susan Pollock, *Ancient Mesopotamia: The Eden That Never Was*, pp. 196–217.

Supplementary Reading:

Joan Aruz, ed., *Art of the First Cities: The Third Millennium B.C. from the Mediterranean to the Indus*, pp. 93–132.

Sir Leonard Woolley, *Digging up the Past.*

Questions to Consider:

1. How does the archaeological evidence found at Ur supplement our understanding of Early Dynastic rulers?

2. What do you think these graves suggest about Mesopotamian understanding of the afterlife?

Lecture Thirteen—Transcript
The Royal Cemetery at Ur

Written sources from the Early Dynastic period have shifted our focus from the temple to the role of the king as the primary leader in the cities of Mesopotamia. In this lecture, we will continue to see the power of the ruler and the occasions when this strength and control were displayed, specifically at his burial. As noted in Lecture Two, one of the most spectacular and widely publicized archaeological discoveries was the cemetery at Ur, excavated in the late 1920s. Ur had been known for many years because of the large ziggurat mound that dominated the site. Visitors to the region had described the site in the 17th century A.D.

Initial excavations began in the mid-19th century when collectors found a number of texts that they sent back to various European museums. After the First World War, Sir Leonard Woolley led a joint expedition sponsored by the British Museum and the University of Pennsylvania. He knew that the temple of Nanna was there—she was the patron deity of the city—and so he had reason to believe that further excavations there would be fruitful. Woolley cleared the ziggurat and continued to explore the temple of Nanna, including portions that had been restored and expanded by the king, Nebuchadnezzar.

In the sixth year of excavations, the team began to uncover a large group of graves that lay below the foundation of these later structures. In the following year, Woolley focused his attention on these graves. Almost 2,000 graves were discovered, but a small group of about 16 burials found in 1927–1929 were so spectacular that newspapers reported their excavation in detail. These royal graves, as they were quickly termed, contained lavish quantities of gold, silver, and semiprecious stones, which were striking enough, but the most surprising feature of the burials was the suggestion that they provided evidence of human sacrifice. No other known burials from Mesopotamia could prepare the excavators for this discovery. Few other archaeological discoveries were as widely publicized; really, only King Tut's intact grave in Egypt discovered in 1922 garnered the same attention. A lot of material exists from this cemetery and we will first discuss a few especially significant objects found to entice you to explore the cemetery further. Then, we'll move to a more detailed view of two graves to study the context as a whole.

We begin with the Standard of Ur, which is in the British Museum. The Standard is a wooden box, about a foot long, and it's covered with lapis lazuli, a creamy white shell, and red limestone. Three rows of scenes are portrayed on both sides of the Standard and there are panels on the side that also show images that we will not discuss in much detail today. The longest side shows a battle. At the top center, a large figure—probably the ruler—faces a row of captives who are nude, with their hands bound. Behind the ruler, a few of his soldiers carry spears and behind them is a chariot being led by donkeys that would have carried the ruler into battle. The second row shows soldiers; some are killing or holding enemies, so this is our closest image of a battle scene. In the bottom row, we see chariots driving over the bodies of the enemies to give a very vivid example of what battle was like.

On the opposite side of the Standard, we move from battle to banquet. Again, on the top, is the largest figure—again, probably the king, presumably the same person. Here he is seated and holding a cup. He wears the fleecy skirt that we have come to expect our rulers to wear. He faces a row of seated males who wear plain skirts with a little bit of fringe on the bottom and they too hold cups. Behind them is a standing male who holds a lyre with a ram-head protome. The lower two registers present men leading animals and bringing food for the banquet. This scene recalls the Uruk Vase from earlier discussions in the course where we had men bringing animals to the priestess of Ur. These distinctions in dress and animal species reveal that the men come from different regions in Mesopotamia. The fish carried by men signal that they come from the southern marshlands and the onagers led by men wearing short skirts with no fringe suggest that they were from northern Mesopotamia. So, for the first time, we see specificity in dress that indicates a regional style or origin. This focus on details of dress will become a typical feature of Mesopotamian art. The Standard was probably stuck on a pole and carried. It would be a very effective symbol for kingship, showing two of his most important functions.

Musical instruments also figure among the unusual artifacts from Ur; since it is very rare for these to survive anywhere in the ancient world, it is worth looking at them quite closely. There are examples of musical instruments in the Iraq Museum, the British Museum, and the University of Pennsylvania Museum. The lyres—these are stringed instruments—are large objects about four or five feet high and they would be held with straps around the shoulders. Most often, these lyres are associated with the bodies of women in the royal cemetery, so we have evidence for female musicians, as well as the male musician that we saw on the Standard of Ur. The lyres are wooden with metal and stone overlay. The wood had decayed, but Sir Leonard Woolley had quickly realized what the objects were. He preserved and consolidated the lyres by pouring plaster over the earth so that the pieces of metal and shell and other stones that decorated the lyre would cling together.

The lyres are decorated with sculptures of animal heads and a bull is especially common. Other shell inlays were attached to the front of the lyre to make it even more decorative. The bull's head is sheathed in gold on the head and horns, and with lapis lazuli used for little tufts of hair over the forehead, at the tips of the bull's horns, and to also create a long, curly beard. The front of the lyre was decorated with a panel of carved shell showing animals and mythical creatures. At the top, a hero clasps two bulls with human heads. The meaning of this is unclear, but it may refer to some story about the Underworld. We don't have any myths that survive that describe this type of scene.

The three lower registers show animals involved in a funeral banquet and they are shown in a little animal band. First, we see a hyena taking the role of a butcher, preparing meat, while a lion carries a jar and a vessel. Below them, a small animal band plays music; a donkey plays a lyre, just like the instrument that we are describing, and even has a little bull's head on the front. A bear stands in front of the lyre, and a little fox is seated before the musician listening to and appreciating the music. The bottom row represents a mythical half-human, half-scorpion figure and a gazelle standing upright and holding beakers. All in all, this is a very festive scene to decorate this musical instrument. Stringed instruments were common at Ur—we have them in all different sizes—and they indicate to us that music was an important part of the funeral ritual.

These two objects give you a taste of what Woolley found. You see how unusual and imaginative they are in comparison to earlier Mesopotamian art. You can see why they would be so intriguing and attract the attention of reporters around the world. Let's move now to study the graves as a whole, to get a better idea of what role these objects would have played in a funeral ritual.

Most Mesopotamian graves were simple pit graves dug into the ground. These graves, the royal graves, were chambers made of brick or stone. So, below the earth there would be a small room created. This is a much more elaborate type of burial and it requires additional labor. We've discussed in several lectures the importance of controlling labor and now the fact that men are used to create these chambers beneath the ground to house a burial is another important sign that a ruler was able to bring together a number of resources—manpower, as well as architecture and other types of resources—that were important for his burial. They would set his grave apart.

These vaulted rectangular chambers were at the bottom of a ramp and inside would be placed a body surrounded by many grave objects and sometimes a vehicle that brought the corpse inside. Oxen or donkeys pulled the sled and their bodies had been found inside the chamber, as well as the corpse. Sometimes, numerous other bodies were found either lying in the chamber or more often outside of it. These were attendants or family members; we can't identify who they are specifically, but we know that there are several bodies that accompany the occupant of the chamber too. Several of these royal tombs were built next to each other. Presumably, we have a situation where the first tomb was built and the successors were buried nearby in a royal district of the cemetery. So, there would be an area where kings and queens and other members of the royal family were buried that was separate and much more elaborate than the rest of the burials of the citizens of Ur.

Within these 16 royal graves, there's a great variation in both the size of the tombs and in the number of bodies buried in them. This is important because it shows us that certain individuals received much larger tombs; perhaps they were wealthier. We'll discuss the meaning of that a little bit later. The royal graves, the 16 royal graves, include both male and female bodies. Most of them were robbed in antiquity, although not completely. We do have this massive quantity of artifacts that were left behind by the looters.

Let's look at a couple of these in more detail. We'll start first with the grave of a male in a chamber tomb built of stone and brick; it was about 12 by 6 feet. It was robbed in antiquity and this complicates our understanding of the objects that survive and the meaning of what the tomb is, but we'll try and figure out what it suggests. Outside of this tomb of the male was the great death pit, as Woolley termed it—a very imaginative phrase that would also help spread attention. This great death pit was intact, so many of the objects that were found associated with this grave come from the burials that were outside.

The bodies of about 60 individuals, mostly women, where stretched out along the ramp. There were six soldiers who carried spears and wore helmets—they were buried right outside of the chamber—and oxen drew two wagons into the chamber tomb. According to Woolley, each of the oxen would have a groom and drivers—a driver on each side—and their bodies were found next to those of the oxen. The women lay in rows along each of the walls and they were very richly adorned with a lot of jewelry. They also found several lyres of the type that I just described nearby the bodies of these women; so, they would have been playing instruments either right before their death or perhaps even in life.

Very near the death pit was the grave of a woman named Pu-Abi and her name was inscribed on a cylinder seal with the title Nin, which means queen. So, here we have our first identified queen from Mesopotamia. She was about 40 and she was buried in a chamber tomb of about the same size as the male, about 12 by 6 feet. Her burial costume was very elaborate. She had a gold headdress made of strips of sheet gold that were woven together to create a cap of glittering leaves and flowers. A comb at the back of her head rose above and had large gold flowers that would sway as she walked. On the head itself was a wreath of flowers, made of gold, lapis, and carnelian, and also a row of willow leaves encircled the head; these were made of gold, as well. Finally, immediately across the forehead was a row of gold rings. Several long ribbons of gold were looped along the side of her head, probably weaving in and out of Pu-Abi's hair or even a wig. We know that Mesopotamian women wore wigs to make their hair even larger and more dominant.

The queen wore a beaded cape that was composed of gold, silver, lapis, carnelian, and agate beads. These long strings of colorful beads would hang from her shoulders to her waist. This was quite heavy, but would also create a very shimmering effect as she walked with strings encircling her body. Beneath the cape was a belt of horizontal beads—mostly lapis with alternating rows of gold, lapis, and carnelian—and a row of gold hoops dangled along the lower edge of the belt. As if this weren't enough, she has other jewelry, as well: no fewer than three necklaces made of gold, some stone beads that would create a necklace over her beaded cape, gold pins, large basket-like earrings made of sheet gold, 10 finger rings—and sometimes multiple rings would be stacked on a single finger—and other miscellaneous adornments.

Three other bodies were found in Pu-Abi's chamber tomb; a male lay near the queen and a female at her feet. These figures did not have a significant number of grave goods buried with them, so it doesn't seem as if they were family members, but rather attendants. The queen had a number of other objects buried with her—numerous gold and silver cups, stone bowls made of agate, furniture inlays that would have decorated perhaps a chair or a stool, and those that survive are silver lion heads with inlaid eyes that are very wide. Also, a number of cosmetic boxes survive that also had decoration on them.

Woolley identified a death pit with Pu-Abi's burial, but subsequent reexamination questions the connection between the bodies found outside the chamber tomb and Pu-Abi's grave. They were created at about the same time, but the death pit lies about six inches higher than the floor of the chamber tomb. So, it may have been made a few years later and may even be linked with another burial. On this ramp leading to the burial chamber of Pu-Abi, were the bodies of several attendants, both male and female, as we saw associated with the male grave. Ten women were set in rows opposite each other and they, too, carried musical instruments, the harps and lyres that we would now expect them to have associated with their bodies. The women wore costumes similar to Pu-Abi, but they were much less elaborate. The headdresses were mostly ribbons of gold; a few had combs with flowers like Pu-Abi wore. There were lots of bead necklaces, several gold necklaces with poplar leaf pendants, gold earrings, and finger rings. But, it's hard not to imagine that this is a lesser version of Pu-Abi's normal dress, so it's a step down. There's a very clear distinction between what the Nin wore and what these attendants wore. The bodies of the men associated with this death pit were also adorned with jewelry—necklaces, rings, and a single earring, in contrast to the two earrings that women wore. They also carried a dagger and a whetstone, so they would have both a defensive weapon and a way to sharpen it always with them, carried at their waist. In addition to the humans found in the grave, the bones of two oxen were identified in the death pit.

These two graves, the goods and the bodies associated with them, are extraordinary. They provide definite evidence for human sacrifice accompanying the burial of a man and a woman of high status—the ruler and the wife of the ruler. The amount of gold and other expensive goods buried in the chamber tombs gives us an idea of what a king and queen would use, and it shows an enormous amount of wealth. These tombs also let us imagine the funeral ritual, which often is not preserved by any archaeological evidence or even any written sources. We can't know if the elaborate costume that Pu-Abi wore was something special, reserved just for the grave, or maybe even represented what she wore on certain ceremonial occasions. But, if it was similar to what she would wear, say, at a religious festival—we know that queens were very closely associated with the temples—then we can see how her dress would set her apart from the rest of the population. With this large headdress with its bouncing flowers of gold and the weighty cape of beads that would make noise, which would move as she did, she would be the center of attention. It's important to consider that dress sets individuals apart by their status. We saw this on the Standard of Ur, where now the men from different regions are shown wearing different costumes. We get the same idea with the costumes that are preserved in the chamber tombs, that Pu-Abi's is significantly richer, more elaborate, and more distinct than those of the attendants outside.

The musical instruments played in a dirge or a hymn and then followed by the death of the attendants—perhaps by some poison, as Woolley suggested—gives us the ultimate symbol of a ruler's power. That he can take his attendants, his courtiers, his subjects with him after death. This ritual suicide could very well have been voluntary. The individuals may have wanted to keep working for their rulers in the afterlife, or perhaps they believed that rulers needed servants in the afterlife, and even compelled them to join them in death. It's hard to reconstruct the particulars of this; we don't even know how they died. Sometimes, as Woolley suggested, this idea of poison is reinforced by cups found in these great death pits, but no trace analysis has survived to reveal any poison. These graves give us remarkable insight into the power of the rulers in the Early Dynastic period. Scholars continue to puzzle over the significance of these tombs, especially since they remain unique discoveries. One of the maxims of the archaeologist is that you always want to find something completely unique that no one has ever found, but then once you do, you don't know how to interpret it. This is exactly the situation with the royal graves at Ur.

Since we have no parallels for this kind of human sacrifice, for even this wealth accompanying the ruler, it's very difficult to get beyond just the general statement that these are wealthy burials of rulers who required the attention of their servants after death. Only one of the inscribed artifacts, a gold vessel with the name of a known ruler, Meskalamdug, was found in a grave chamber. Pu-Abi's cylinder seal was found right outside of the chamber. Meskalamdug's vessel was found in the chamber and that does help reinforce the idea that these are rulers. It is possible that some of the gifts were given by other rulers rather than actually belonging to the people in the chamber. So, one theory is that it is not only kings and queens buried in these chamber tombs, but that we also have members of the elite that were especially favored by a king or a queen. To me, this does not seem especially convincing because we don't get a lot of information about a ruling elite—an important group of governors, or military leaders, or even bureaucrats—who were especially important to a king in the Early Dynastic period. The focus is solely on the ruler.

One of the biggest puzzles about the royal graves at Ur revolves around this practice of ritual murder or suicide. Why was this act considered necessary at this time? As I said, these graves and the death pits associated with them are unparalleled at any other time in Mesopotamian history. It's a little difficult to understand the meaning, but we do get some hint of a possible explanation in the story of the death of Gilgamesh. You remember I told you that, in addition to the Epic of Gilgamesh, there are also other stories that described this king of Uruk. The story about his death does record that he was buried with the female members of his family, as well some courtiers. It also describes Gilgamesh building his chamber tomb before his death; he realized he was near his death and so he begins construction on his tomb. Outside of Mesopotamia, there are examples of ritual murder in other cultures. It is not a common feature in that it lasts for several generations, but anthropologists stress that it can occur in a time of great crisis in a community, perhaps during a plague or famine. It is possible that this scenario might explain the Ur graves. We don't have any other written sources that could describe what sort of crisis existed, but a famine may not appear in the texts. You'll remember that most texts from the Early Dynastic period only discuss the actions of a king. And so, he would not be eager to discuss what he would see as a plague or a famine or some divine occurrence that would interfere with his reign. The ritual suicide may be our only evidence for some greater widespread problem in Mesopotamia. The wealth of these graves is overwhelming, and if we add to that the evidence for mass suicide or murder on the death of a ruler, we do get a real sense of the power of a king and a queen.

In the next lecture, we will meet Sargon, a king of Akkad who became so powerful that he united northern and southern Mesopotamia for the first time under his rule. So, we begin to see, as we move from one generation of kings who set themselves apart in their burials, next we see a king who expands his military might and controls a much larger area than we've seen to this time.

Lecture Fourteen
The Akkadians

Scope:

In this lecture, we move from the kings of cities to the first ruler who could legitimately claim his mastery over northern and southern Mesopotamia. The rise of Sargon of Akkad (r. c. 2334–2279 B.C.) shows the dominance of northern Mesopotamia, or Akkad, over Sumer in the south and the beginning of a new dynasty. Although we have some contemporary sources for Sargon's rule, the majority of our texts were written much later, when he had become a legendary figure worthy of emulation. These sources claim to be copies of original texts inscribed on Akkadian monuments, but it is likely that later rulers embellished the accounts to serve their own purposes. It is a challenge to sort out the facts of Sargon's rule from these anachronistic sources, but they attest to the lingering influence of this era in Mesopotamian history.

Outline

I. One of the most striking stories about Sargon's early life is his birth legend, which is reported in an 8th-century B.C. Neo-Assyrian source.

   A. The legend reports that Sargon was the son of a priestess and an unknown father. His mother placed him in a basket and set him afloat on a river, which brought Sargon to Aqqi, the "drawer of water."

   B. The Sumerian king list records Sargon's birth as well, describing him in different versions as the son of a gardener or as the cupbearer of the king of Kish, Ur-Zababa. Sargon overthrew, and likely assassinated, Ur-Zababa to take the throne of Kish and expand his rule.

   C. Sargon's story, even if it was recorded later, would have preceded the Old Testament story of Moses, and it attests to the importance of rivers in Mesopotamia and Egypt.

   D. Other stories about Sargon relate a dream that he had while still in the service of Ur-Zababa; according to the story, Sargon dreamed that Inanna killed Ur-Zababa, and this divine sign could justify his assassination of the king.

E. Sargon's Akkadian name, Sharru-ken, means the "true" or "legitimate" king, an overstatement that suggests that he had no real claim to the throne.

  1. After taking the throne of Kish, Sargon quickly attacked and defeated the king of Uruk, Lugalzagesi.

  2. This king had noted in an inscription on a silver vessel that he controlled the land to the west and east, indicating a change in military objective from the small-scale border conflicts we have seen, such as that between Umma and Lagash.

II. Sargon's main accomplishments stemmed from his military achievements, which took him east to Iran, apparently as far west as Lebanon, north into Anatolia, and to the south of Mesopotamia.

A. Inscriptions contemporary to Sargon's reign note that the god Dagan (the god of grain) gave him the upper Euphrates regions, including Ebla and Mari, trading cities in Syria, and that he controlled the lands west to the Cedar Mountains (of Lebanon).

B. Later stories about Sargon offer more detailed descriptions of his campaigns, but these may not be especially reliable.

  1. A partially preserved epic poem about Sargon reports his skill and ambition in battle.

  2. When Sargon arrives and successfully besieges the city, his enemy concedes to him, saying, "Your opponents' hearts are seared; they are terrified and left paralyzed with fear." The mere presence of later Assyrian rulers was believed to cause an opponent's city or army to immediately surrender.

  3. As always, divine support was necessary for victory; Sargon claimed both divine support and a close relationship with Inanna.

  4. Sargon's most memorable claim is that he washed his spear in the sea of the Persian Gulf. Later rulers, including his Assyrian namesake, Sargon II, emulated this act in direct imitation.

  5. One of the most intriguing contemporary texts refers to Sargon eating bread with 5,400 men every day. This could be a reference to a standing army; if so, this is the first recorded army in history.

III. Scholars debate whether Sargon's Akkad was the first known empire; the issue revolves around modern definitions of *empire* and does not relate to ancient conceptions of kingship or political power.

    A. Modern scholars identify an empire based on a combination of certain characteristics:

        1. A deliberate policy of territorial expansion.

        2. A coherent system of governance.

        3. The visible expression and extent of a ruler's power.

    B. Some scholars agree with the idea that Sargon's Akkad fits this definition, while others believe that the concept is not fulfilled until the Assyrians create an empire in the 1st millennium B.C.

    C. The obstacle to identifying Sargon's kingship as the first empire is that written sources do not convey a deliberate plan to expand the territory or to provide a coherent system of governance.

IV. The emphasis on military success in the surviving texts relating to Sargon complicates our study of the bureaucracy that controlled the Akkadian territories.

    A. Sargon founded a new capital, Akkad or Agade, from which to rule his lands. This capital, as yet undiscovered, is thought to be near or beneath Baghdad.

    B. The founding of a new city is contrary to what we have come to expect in Mesopotamia, where the old cities have such a rich history. What would be the benefits of a new capital city?

        1. As an illegitimate ruler, Sargon could use a new city to invoke a new era, surrounding himself with temples and art that would celebrate his rule without awkward references to earlier rulers that he overthrew. Later rulers will also set up new capital cities; such foundations are always important events described in the texts.

        2. We have little Akkadian architecture and cannot evaluate any changes that this new dynasty may have represented in its public architecture. Sargon may have used traditional forms of architecture to show his connection to the past.

3. Akkadian was made the official language of the royal bureaucracy. This shift in language could be interpreted as a way for Sargon to govern his lands in a consistent manner.

4. We know that he sent *ensis* (governors), some of them his sons, others presumably his trusted officials, to oversee cities.

5. Sargon established a uniform system of weights and measurements that was especially useful for levying tribute or paying other obligations to the state.

V. One of the most significant decisions that Sargon made to consolidate his power was to install his daughter as a priestess.

   A. Enheduanna was the high priestess of the moon god Nanna at Ur, which would give her control over the temple lands and other property controlled by this powerful cult in southern Mesopotamia.

   B. She may also have served in some priestly function at Uruk, which would represent a unification of these powerful religious centers.

   C. While serving as priestess, Enheduanna composed hymns to the goddess Inanna and many other deities, which makes her the first known author in history. The songs extol Inanna's strength and wisdom, placing her as a critical member of the assemblies of the gods.

   D. An alabaster disk found at Ur, now in the University of Pennsylvania Museum, shows Enheduanna making a sacrifice to Inanna.

   E. After Sargon, it became traditional for a ruler who claimed allegiance of more than one city to also place a daughter in this cultic position. This would give a ruler important religious justification for his claims to control southern Mesopotamia and the lucrative temple estates at Ur.

VI. Sargon ruled for 55 years; the length of his reign undoubtedly contributed to its success because it allowed him to ensure succession after establishing his control.

A. Despite Sargon's success, a later source notes that all the lands revolted against him late in life; he was besieged in Akkad, but he defeated his opponents. There would be another revolt immediately after Sargon's death, and we will see that the period of succession was often difficult.

B. Rimush (r. 2278–2270 B.C.), Sargon's son and successor, ruled for only nine years before he was assassinated. The sources claim that his servants "killed him with their tablets."

C. His brother, Manishtushu (r. 2269–2255 B.C.), took the throne, ruled for another 14 years, and seems to have been an active campaigner, crossing the Persian Gulf to gain control of silver mines. While he was away, Akkadian dominance of northern Mesopotamia (Ebla and Mari) weakened, and Akkadian access to the metal trading routes was cut off.

D. Sargon and his successors seem to have desired control of these trade routes more so than agricultural lands. When these routes were cut off, the kings often had to return to the region and reestablish their control. This fact suggests that the Akkadians lacked a strong governance and that local movements may have been intensely independent.

VII. Sargon was the first ruler to unite northern and southern Mesopotamia, setting a precedent for his successors to establish regional control, rather than control over one or two cities and their lands.

A. He further reinforced his power by placing his daughter in the position of high priestess at Ur, which gave him critical support in southern Mesopotamia and religious validation for his rule.

B. At the end of his rule, and during the reign of his immediate successors, indications of rebellion and unrest show the difficulty of any larger entity in maintaining leadership over these fiercely independent city-states.

C. In the next lecture, we will examine how Sargon's grandson, Naram-Sin, attempted a different form of political and social control in Mesopotamia that focused on religion.

Essential Reading:

Sabina Franke, "Kings of Akkad: Sargon and Naram-Sin," in *CANE*, vol. II, pp. 831–842.

Benjamin R. Foster, *From Distant Days: Myths, Tales and Poetry of Ancient Mesopotamia*, pp. 165–170.

Supplementary Reading:

Jean-Daniel Forest, "The State: The Process of State Formation as Seen from Mesopotamia," in Susan Pollock and Reinhard Bernbeck, eds., *Archaeologies of the Middle East: Critical Perspectives*, pp. 184–206.

Questions to Consider:

1. Do you think that Sargon established an empire? How would you define an empire?

2. Why do you think that later rulers were so enraptured by Sargon?

Lecture Fourteen—Transcript
The Akkadians

In the previous lecture, we examined the exceptional discovery of the royal cemetery at Ur and considered how the ruling elite expressed their power in funeral rituals. We discussed the lavish grave goods—including jewelry, musical instruments, and cups of gold and silver—that comforted the dead rulers, and human sacrifice is also attested in the royal burials. This unparalleled ritual demonstrates a ruler's control over the life and death of his or her people, but so far is limited to the late Early Dynastic period, and may have had a specific social, political, or economic purpose that did not occur again.

In this lecture, we move from the kings of cities to the first ruler who could legitimately claim his mastery over both northern and southern Mesopotamia. The rise of Sargon, who ruled from 2334–2279 B.C., shows the dominance of northern Mesopotamia or Akkad over Sumer in the south, which has been the focus of most of our discussions so far. It also shows the beginning of a new dynasty. While we have some contemporary sources for Sargon's rule, the majority of our sources were written much later when Sargon had become a legendary figure worthy of emulation. These later sources claim to be copies of the original texts inscribed on Akkadian monuments, but it is likely that later rulers embellished the accounts to serve their own purposes. Perhaps they, too, were trying to control both the north and south and they wanted some historical precedent to justify their claim, so they would focus on Sargon and make his rule seem even more powerful than it might have been. Even the art of Sargon and some of his Akkadian successors was found not in Akkad, where it was originally displayed, but in Iran, where an Elamite king had them transported to his palace in the 12th century B.C. to be displayed as spoils of war after he had invaded southern Mesopotamia. So, he took the objects back to enjoy looking at in his own palace.

It is a challenge to sort out the facts of Sargon's rule from these anachronistic sources, but they attest to the lingering influence of this era in Mesopotamian history. One of the most striking stories about Sargon's early life is his birth legend, which is reported in an 8th-century B.C. neo-Assyrian source. The legend reports that Sargon was the son of a priestess and some unknown father; the father is never mentioned in any versions of this story. The story claims: "My mother was a high priestess, I did not know my father…my mother conceived me, she bore me in secret, she placed me in a reed basket, she sealed my hatch with pitch. She left me to the river…the river carried me off, it brought me to Aqqi, drawer of water." Aqqi, then, had Sargon work in an orchard. It was presumably a royal orchard because Sargon comes into contact with the king, and we'll get to that in just a moment.

The Sumerian king list records Sargon's birth, as well, describing him in different versions as the son of a gardener or as the cupbearer of the King of Kish, Ur-Zababa.

It is certain that Sargon overthrew and probably assassinated Ur-Zababa to take the throne of Kish and, from there, expanded his rule. These early stories may seem somewhat familiar to you, especially the story of the baby bound in a reed basket floating along the river. Sargon's story, even if it is a later version, would have appeared before the legend of Moses recorded in the Old Testament, but it shows the importance of the rivers both in Mesopotamia and also in the Nile.

Getting back to Sargon's early life, other stories record that Sargon had a dream while he was still in the service of Ur-Zababa, the king of Kish. According to the story, Sargon dreamt that the goddess Inanna killed Ur-Zababa, thus justifying the gods' displeasure with the ruler. Therefore, if Sargon actually did assassinate Ur-Zababa, he would just be the agent of the gods as predicted in his dream. There's a great detail from this story that shows the importance of diplomatic secrecy. The story reports: "In those days, writing on tables did exist, but clay envelopes did not exist. King Ur-Zababa wrote a tablet for Sargon, creature of the gods, which would cause his own death, and dispatched it to Lugalzagesi in Uruk," another king whom Sargon will come into contact with. So, we see that this is sort of an early espionage story where Ur-Zababa may have felt some threat from Sargon and he wrote about it trying to get help from a co-ruler in Uruk, Lugalzagesi. Sargon saw it because it was not sealed in an envelope.

Sargon's Akkadian name, Sharru-Kin, means the true or legitimate king—an overstatement that suggests that he, in fact, had no real claim to the throne. After coming to the throne of Kish, Sargon quickly attacked and defeated the powerful king of Uruk,

Lugalzagesi, who just reported as an ally of Ur-Zababa. Lugalzagesi led a coalition of 50 *ensis*. You remember that an *ensi* is some sort of governor of a city. You may also recall that we met Lugalzagesi when he made very splashy dedications to Enlil at Nippur. Lugalzagesi noted in an inscription on a silver vessel that he controlled the land east and west, and this was a change in goal from the small-scale border conflicts, such at that that we discussed between Umma and Lagash. Rulers are now trying to not just get more agricultural land, but to control a territory.

Sargon's main accomplishments stemmed from his military achievements. These expeditions took him east to Iran, apparently as far west as Lebanon, to the north in Anatolia, and finally, to the south of Mesopotamia, which allowed him to unite the two regions. Inscriptions contemporary to Sargon's reign note that the god Dagan, who is the god of grain, gave him the upper Euphrates regions— including Ebla and Mari, the trading cities in Syria that we have discussed—and that he controlled the land west to the Cedar Mountains, which would be Lebanon. Keep in mind that in previous lectures we've talked about diplomatic connections between Mesopotamia and Ebla and Mari. Now, this has turned to a more military control of the regions with the reign of Sargon. The copperhead of an Akkadian ruler, perhaps Sargon, from the Iraq Museum that we discussed in the first lecture was found at Nineveh in northern Mesopotamia.

Later stories about Sargon offer much more detailed descriptions of his campaigns, but these, as already discussed, may not be especially reliable. A partially preserved epic poem about Sargon reports both his skill and his ambition in battle. A ruler of Anatolian area tells a group of Mesopotamian merchants that Sargon would never travel so far to protect them. He says: "Sargon will not come as far as we are. Riverbank and high water will surely prevent him, the massive mountain will surely make a reed thicket." When Sargon did arrive and successfully besieged the city, his enemy conceded to him saying, "no doubt your gods…brought your soldiers across. What lands could rival Akkad? What king could rival you? …Your opponents' hearts are seared, they are terrified, and left paralyzed with fear." I want you to keep this in mind as we discuss later rulers, especially the Assyrians, who believed that just the presence of the king could cause an opponent's city or army to immediately surrender. We get the first hints of that idea with Sargon. As always, divine support of a king's rule was necessary and Sargon claimed that as well. "When Enlil had given the rulership and kingship from the south as far as the highlands to Sargon, king of Akkad—at that time, holy Inanna established the sanctuary of Akkad as her celebrated woman's domain." We see that Sargon and Inanna have an especially close relationship. He draws on her quite frequently.

One of Sargon's most memorable claims is that he washed his spear in the sea of the Persian Gulf. Later rulers—including his Assyrian namesake, Sargon II—emulated this act in direct imitation of Sargon's success. So, they're using this symbolic act to recall the past. Another intriguing text refers to Sargon eating bread with 5,400 men every day. This is a contemporary text and it seems likely that it's a reference to a standing army; if so, this is the first recorded army in history. Scholars debate whether Sargon's Akkad was the first known empire, and the issue revolves around the modern definitions of empire and doesn't relate in any way to the ancient conceptions of kingship or political power. This is a topic that intrigues historians and political scientists; therefore, it can allow us to reflect on the events of this prehistoric period.

Modern scholars identify an empire based on a combination of certain characteristics and these change depending on which scholar is defining an empire. Most require a deliberate policy of territorial expansion, a coherent system of governance, and the visible expression of a ruler's power. Some scholars agree with the idea that Sargon's Akkad fits this definition, while others believe that the concept is not fulfilled until the Assyrians create an empire in the 1st millennium B.C. The main sticking point for identifying Sargon's kingship as the first empire is that written sources do not convey a deliberate plan to expand the territory or even necessarily provide a coherent system of governance. You can think about this and about your idea of empire as we continue our study, and you can decide which Mesopotamian culture best fits your own definition of empire. My opinion changes pretty much every time I teach the course as to whether this was the first empire or not. One problem with coming to an understanding of how Sargon ruled his empire is that most of the sources that we can date most closely to Sargon's reign focus on his military activities rather than any sort of bureaucratic control over the Akkadian territory.

Sargon founded a new capital, Akkad or Agade, from which to rule his lands. This capital has not been discovered to date. It's either near or maybe even under the city of Baghdad. If we think about this act, we should be somewhat surprised that there's a new city being founded. It's contrary to what we come to expect in Mesopotamia, where old cities have such a rich history. And so, as we consider why Sargon would have founded a new city, let's think about what the benefits would be. This takes us directly to Sargon's personal history as some one who does not have a legitimate claim to the throne. Sargon could use a new city to invoke a new era. He could surround himself with temples, art that could celebrate him without any awkward references to earlier rulers that he overthrew who had a legitimate claim to the throne. Later rulers will also establish new capital cities; it's always an important event, one that they describe in great detail in their texts and one that we will take note of as we come across them.

Probably because Akkad has not been discovered, we have little Akkadian architecture, so we can't evaluate any changes that this new dynasty may have represented in public architecture. I'm guessing that Sargon would have used very traditional forms of architecture as a way to show his connection to the past, but until we find Akkad, we won't know that for certain. Akkadian was the official language of the royal bureaucracy, and so we see a language shift for the first time in the history that we've discussed. Remember cuneiform was a script; it was used to record Sumerian, but the symbols could be used for any language. We saw this at Ebla, where the local language, Eblaite, was recorded in cuneiform script. This shift in language could be interpreted as a way to govern his lands in a consistent manner, so this might help us identify Akkad as an empire, but that is debatable. We know that Sargon sent *ensis*—some of them were his sons, others presumably trusted officials—to oversee different cities in the south, especially. That's where the texts survive. Sargon also established a uniform system of weights and measurements that was especially useful for levying tribute or other obligations to the state. It standardized what goods were necessary for a city or region to provide.

One of the most significant decisions that Sargon made to consolidate his power was to install his daughter as a priestess. Enheduanna was the high priestess of the moon god Nanna at Ur, and this would give her control over the temple lands in Ur and also other property controlled by the cult in southern Mesopotamia. She may also have served some priestly function at Uruk, which could represent a unification of these powerful religious centers, and so we see Sargon as the military leader and his daughter becoming a very prominent religious leader in different cities—so we have the same priestess for multiple cities and multiple cults. By definition, that would unify worship. While serving as priestess, Enheduanna composed hymns to the goddess Inanna and many other deities, and this makes her the first known author in history. It's nice that it's a woman. The songs extol Inanna's strength and wisdom, placing her as a critical member in the assemblies of the gods. Remember Sargon also had this close connection to Inanna, so it's not surprising that his daughter would be focused on her cult. Inanna glories in battle: "In her joyful heart she performs the song of death on the plain. She performs the song in her heart. She washes their weapons with blood and gore, …Axes smash heads, spears penetrate and maces are covered in blood."

Somewhat less martial in tone, Inanna also has enormous power. Enheduanna writes in another poem:

> I am Enheduanna, the high priestess of the moon goddess…my lady, let me proclaim your magnificence in all lands, and your glory! Let me praise your ways and greatness! Who rivals you in divinity? Queen of all given powers, unveiled clear light, unfailing woman wearing brilliance, cherished in heaven and earth…my queen of fundamental forces, you lift up the elements…you gather in powers…like the storm god you howl, grain wilts on the ground, swollen flood rushing down the mountain, you are Inanna, supreme in heaven and earth…

If you recall our discussion of Mesopotamian deities, you see the unrivaled power and also how vicious a goddess could be. All of this is described in these poems. There are also phrases that recall the power of the king: "the king too is unrivaled in power." He's an enormous military force and so any text from Sargon's era or those of his successors that uses this phrasing may have been a deliberate way to connect the king to the power of the gods.

An Alabaster disk found at Ur and now in the University of Pennsylvania Museum shows Enheduanna making a sacrifice to

Inanna. An inscription on the reverse identifies the priestess, so we're sure that this is Sargon's daughter. She stands in a row with a nude male priest and two other women. Enheduanna is distinct from these other figures by her larger size—her head reaches the top of the register, the carved part of the disk—and her much more elaborate costume. All of the figures stand before an altar and a stepped structure that looks very much like a ziggurat. After Sargon, it became traditional that a ruler who claimed the allegiance of more than one city would also place his daughter in the cultic position. This gives the ruler an important religious justification for his claims to control southern Mesopotamia, as well as controlling the lucrative temple estates at Ur. Previous priestesses would not be expelled or removed when a new ruler came to power, but when they died, the ruler who was in charge would put his daughter in this position. It shows that the religious function was important and, even though we can see that it would be used for political purposes, it was not something that the ruler could do without a vacancy in the power of the priestess.

Sargon ruled for 55 years and the length of his reign undoubtedly contributed to its success because it helps allow him to ensure succession after establishing his control. It also allows him to establish a personality and this fear that he supposedly inspired in his enemies. Especially if he was the leader of the first standing army and one that was definitely very successful, this would also solidify his position and make him seem important and someone who was going to be in place for a long time. Despite Sargon's success militarily, a later source describes that all of the lands revolted against him late in life, and so they besieged him in Akkad. Thus, not only did they try to overthrow his rule presumably by overthrowing the governors he had sent to rule over the cities, but they also moved against him. Sargon defeated this rebellion and also traveled on campaigns to make sure that other rebellions were put down. Immediately after Sargon's death there will be another series of revolts and this is the first time where we have evidence for the period of succession of a ruler as he's trying to establish a dynasty. It was often very difficult and would inspire regions or cities or other rulers to try and take back their own power. This will be especially true in the 1st millennium.

Rimush, Sargon's son and successor, ruled for only nine years before he was assassinated. He ruled from 2278–2270 B.C. The sources claim that his servants "killed him with their tablets," which is a very mysterious way of assassinating a king; no one else died in this particular matter. It's a little hard to imagine these cuneiform tablets being wielded as weapons, so you'll have to think about that and how a palace revolt would actually work.

His brother, Manishtushu, who ruled from 2269–2255 B.C., took the throne and ruled for another 14 years. He seems to have been a very active campaigner, crossing the Persian Gulf in order to gain control of silver mines. But, while he was away, Akkadian control of northern Mesopotamia, the cities of Ebla and Mari, weakened. This cut off Akkadian access to the metal trading routes that were so important. These constant revolts and the areas that the Akkadians tried to control were not agricultural territories, as we saw in earlier periods of history, but they were important regions that provided access to major trade routes, especially metal. It seems that Sargon and his Akkadian dynasty wanted control of these trade routes more than the land itself. When these routes were cut off, the king would go back and try to open them up. The fact that the Akkadians have to keep returning to the areas that they supposedly controlled shows that they did not have a very strong governance system in place or that local movements of independence was very deeply rooted. Remember I discussed one of the problems we have with interpreting historical texts is that they always describe the ruler as completely controlling the enemy that he has taken on and leaving the enemy defeated and crushed; the cities are often described as being utterly destroyed. But, when a ruler has to keep going back as Sargon did—so, here we have the first and most powerful military ruler in history that we can discuss in detail—even he has to keep going back to regions to try and dominate them and to prevent them from losing their control.

Sargon was the first ruler to unite northern and southern Mesopotamia and he set a precedent for his successors to establish regional control rather than control over just one or two cities and their lands. He further reinforced this power by placing his daughter in the position of high priestess at Ur and perhaps even control of other cities. This gave him critical support in southern Mesopotamia and also religious validation for his rule. At the end of his rule and during the reign of his successors, there are numerous indications of rebellion and unrest, and it shows the difficulty of any larger entity maintaining leadership over these fiercely independent city-states. Remember that each city believed it was the home of the gods and that is one reason why, I think, it was so difficult for a king to establish control over multiple cities. They each had a long history, unless the ruler decided to create a new capital city, and a history that involved self-rule. And so, as one man tries to break down this loyalty, it becomes very difficult. We'll see that Sargon's grandson, Naram-Sin, tried a new method of establishing control that also focused on religion. Since religion is the aspect of Mesopotamia that remains uniform throughout the entire period that we discuss, it would be a very effective tool for a ruler to use to try and shift those old alliances to a new way of thinking.

Lecture Fifteen
Ideology of Kingship—Naram-Sin and Gudea

Scope:

The reign of Naram-Sin marks the high point of Akkadian rule, with the boundaries of the empire reaching their greatest extent. With Naram-Sin, for the first time, we see a ruler worshipped as divine during his lifetime, a radical change in the conception of kingship. The art of the era shows important developments in the Mesopotamian representation of the king and in depictions of the human figure. The success of Naram-Sin's reign did not last, and later writers represent him as suffering from personal pride that brought disaster to himself and the collapse of Akkadian rule. Once the Akkadians were removed from power, city-states again became politically important, as they had been in the Early Dynastic era. In Lagash, in southern Mesopotamia, a new ruler arose, Gudea, who was the first of a dynasty that would govern during an exceptionally wealthy and peaceful era. The portraits of Gudea rejected the new way in which Naram-Sin had represented himself and returned to a more traditional style.

Outline

I. The rule of Naram-Sin (c. 2254–2218 B.C.), the grandson of Sargon, became as notorious for its supposed failure in later generations as his predecessor's rule was praised. But a closer look shows that the later sources that condemned Naram-Sin exaggerate the historical situation; he was, in fact, a strong leader who expanded the borders of Akkadian control.

II. As we begin to look in detail at rulers in the ancient Near East, we need to briefly discuss the chronology of the region, which is quite unsettled.

    A. We have a good idea of the sequence of rulers; that is, we know who ruled and in what order, but specific dates come from various sources (astrological texts, political texts from other countries) and are by no means consistent.

    B. Assyrian documents record a solar eclipse that occurred on June 15, 763 B.C. From that confirmed date we get very close dates for 1st-millennium B.C. history, but the 3rd and 2nd millennia are much more uncertain.

C. Three different chronologies have been established for Mesopotamian history—a high, middle, and low chronology. We have used the middle chronology in this course, but questions remain about all three systems.

III. Naram-Sin succeeded his father, Manishtushu, and ruled for 46 years, during which time he faced revolts in Mesopotamia and challenges on its borders, often repeating campaigns that Sargon had originally undertaken.

A. During Naram-Sin's rule, the Akkadians controlled the area of Elam in southwest Iran, Sumer, Akkad, and part of northern Syria. Most of the evidence for these borders comes from dedications with inscriptions recording campaigns or boundary markers set up in these regions.

B. Naram-Sin's expeditions were focused on controlling trade routes, for example, to ensure access to the Indus Valley and to northern Syria. In Syria, at Tell Brak, bricks from a monumental building are stamped with Naram-Sin's name, showing his sponsorship and indicating that the Akkadians intended to settle there.

C. At some point in his reign, Naram-Sin adopted a new title, "King of the Four Quarters of the World," which essentially defined him as ruler of the known world.

D. One of the most significant revolts against Akkadian rule came from an unusually strong alliance of southern city-states, which Naram-Sin shattered. After this revolt, Naram-Sin chose to deify himself, introducing a new concept of rulership.

E. For the latter part of his reign, the sign for a deity was placed before his name in all written sources. This was an unprecedented act for a Mesopotamian ruler, and it may explain the later hostility toward him, but the immediate reaction of his subjects remains unclear.

IV. Naram-Sin also portrayed himself in a new and radical way in the visual arts. A limestone relief sculpture called the Victory

Stele of Naram-Sin, now in the Louvre, shows the king as victor over a mountain tribe, the Lullubi in Elam.

A. Some aspects of the image are familiar to us: Naram-Sin is larger than any other figures on the stele and the focus of attention; he is shown in battle, leading his troops as a good king was required to do.

B. The stele also shows several innovations. For example, instead of the usual registers that frame a scene, the entire background of this sculpture is employed.

   1. Naram-Sin has defeated a mountain tribe and is shown climbing up a mountain, with his army behind him.

   2. The usual motif of the victor crushing his enemies beneath his feet is retained, although these opponents are not nude but wear short skirts. To the viewer, this might convey the idea that the battle is ongoing.

   3. The most important change in this representation is that Naram-Sin is shown wearing the horned helmet that was reserved for the gods. His divinity is underscored by the fact that no other gods are shown on the stele, although they are represented symbolically by stars.

   4. The rendering of Naram-Sin's body also reveals his divinity. He wears a short skirt that falls between his legs; his right arm is bare and quite muscular. The image emphasizes his strength and resembles typical artistic depictions of gods and heroes.

C. One theory explains Naram-Sin's self-deification as an attempt by the Akkadian king to break down or divert the population's strong identification with individual cities and their own ruling elite and gods.

V. We don't know how successful Naram-Sin's strategy was, and later written sources express clear discomfort with his claim of divinity. His arrogance and impiety were used to explain the collapse of Akkadian rule.

A. A text called "The Curse of Akkad" describes the fall of the Akkadians, blaming Naram-Sin and his impiety for the collapse. This inscription is supposedly copied from a stele set up by Naram-Sin.

B. According to this source, Enlil sent Naram-Sin a dream, in which the god revealed a terrifying future for Akkad; Naram-Sin refused to share the dream with anyone but, instead, hid in his palace for seven years. He then attacked the temple of Enlil at Nippur.

C. Enlil's rage was intense, and he sent a mountain tribe, the Gutians, to retaliate. The motif of foreign tribes acting as agents of the gods was a common explanation for a change in power in Mesopotamian literature.

D. These tribes are often from the mountains or deserts, where development of cities would not be possible. As we discussed in an earlier lecture, the geography of some parts of Mesopotamia would have promoted smaller, more independent communities.

E. Texts characterize these mountain tribes as uncivilized, with an animal-like appearance. All the phrases used to describe the Gutians separate them from normal daily life. In this way, the texts dehumanize the invaders, just as visual representations show the complete subjugation of the enemy through nudity.

VI. The Akkadian Empire would last for at least another 20 years after the death of Naram-Sin, belying the image of swift divine retribution against the ruler. Little archaeological evidence of destruction or major disruptions in this period has been found that would confirm "The Curse of Akkad"; we must be satisfied with suggestions of rebellion.

A. Sharkali-Sharri (r. c. 2217–2193), the king of Akkad who succeeded Naram-Sin, gave up the title of "King of the Four Quarters" during his reign; this change in nomenclature seems to indicate a general withdrawal of the kingdom of Akkad to the north.

B. The Gutians returned and were more successful, briefly controlling southern Mesopotamia. Sharkali-Sharri's reign seems to have been largely concerned with defense against internal and external threats.

C. After Sharkali-Sharri's reign came a period in which there was no leader. The Sumerian king list for this period reads: "Who was king? Who was not king?" Considering that the king list was focused on supporting the office of kingship, this concession to the chaos of the era is significant.

D. In Mesopotamia, city-states regained their autonomy from Akkadian control; no single power controlled multiple cities in the region.

E. After the fall of the Akkadians, we refer to southern and central Mesopotamia as Babylonia. This name reflects the existence of a consistent political unit (the city-state), as well as religious, linguistic, and cultural accord. Babylonia will continue as an identifiable and distinct region almost until the end of the period we are studying.

VII. The city-state of Lagash in Sumer benefited from the disruption at the end of the Akkadian period and was one of the states that reestablished self-rule by the late 3rd millennium B.C.

A. Gudea, the second ruler of the dynasty that took control of Lagash after the fall of Akkad, is not an especially noteworthy ruler, but the chance discovery of several statues of the king have made him one of the most recognizable rulers in Mesopotamian history.

B. The statues of Gudea emphasize the ruler's piety and humility before the gods. He clasps his hands in an attitude familiar from earlier Mesopotamian votive sculpture, in opposition to Naram-Sin's representations of himself.

C. In contrast to his bearded, long-haired Akkadian predecessors, Gudea is smooth-shaven, and his hair is short or tucked beneath a cap in a style similar to that worn by priests. Nonetheless, the statues retain the focus on his physical strength.

D. Relief sculptures depict Gudea engaged in building temples, and one even shows an architectural plan of a temple that he sponsored.

E. These images reinforce Gudea's concern for the traditional role of the king. In an era marked by political and economic fragmentation and change, a king who focused his attention on local needs would be appreciated.

F. The sculpted portraits that we have discussed illustrate the different ways that these two rulers presented themselves, reflected their broader message to their people, and served as visual bookends for the history of this period. Naram-Sin's self-divination, although perhaps radical at the time, will be adopted by the next great dynasty that we will meet, the Ur III rulers.

Essential Reading:

Joan Aruz, ed., *Art of the First Cities: The Third Millennium B.C. from the Mediterranean to the Indus*, pp. 417–433.

Benjamin R. Foster, *From Distant Days: Myths, Tales and Poetry of Ancient Mesopotamia*, pp. 171–177.

Supplementary Reading:

Irene Winter, "Sex, Rhetoric and the Public Monument: The Alluring Body of Naram-Sin of Agade," in N. B. Kampen and B. Bergmann, eds., *Sexuality in Ancient Art*, pp. 11–26.

Questions to Consider:

1. What political benefits would Naram-Sin gain by presenting himself as a god?

2. How does Gudea present himself differently?

Lecture Fifteen—Transcript
Ideology of Kingship—Naram-Sin and Gudea

The rule of Naram-Sin, the grandson of Sargon, became as notorious for its supposed failure in later generations as his predecessor's rule was praised. A closer look at the evidence for Naram-Sin's rule shows that the later sources that condemned him exaggerated the historical situation and that Naram-Sin was, in fact, a strong leader who expanded the borders of Akkadian control during his reign. He was certainly as successful militarily as his grandfather had been. As we look at what we can extract from the contemporary records of Naram-Sin's rule, we will consider what actions would have caused such offense to later rulers.

Before I get into Naram-Sin's rule, I want to talk to you briefly about chronology. I've been giving some very specific dates in this course and I'm sure that I seem very certain about them. In fact, the chronology for the ancient Near East is quite unsettled. We have a good idea of the sequence of rulers, so we know who ruled in what order, but we get the dates from different types of sources. Sometimes we get them from astronomical texts; sometimes from other political events with countries such as Egypt, so we have a chronology for Egypt that we reconcile with whoever happens to be ruling in Mesopotamia at the time. The day of June 15, 763, a solar eclipse occurred and was recorded in Assyrian documents. From that specific date, which has been confirmed, we get very close dates for 1st-millennium history. But, the 3rd millennium and the 2nd millennium are much more uncertain. There are three different chronologies that have been established for Mesopotamian history— a high, a middle, and a low—and they all have problems. I have been using the middle chronology. Just as a compromise, there are as many difficulties with those dates as there are with the others, but we have to go with something, so I have chosen the middle chronology. If you are reading a history of the Near East, you may find that the dates can be off by as much as 40 years or so.

Let's turn back to Naram-Sin. Naram-Sin succeeded his father Manishtushu and ruled for 46 years, from 2254–2218 B.C., another of those very specific dates. During this time, Naram-Sin had to face revolts in Mesopotamia and challenges on its borders. He often repeated campaigns that Sargon had originally undertaken. Unlike the other Akkadian rulers that we know existed in this dynasty,

Naram-Sin and Sargon both were great military leaders and they traveled the farthest of any of the rulers. During Naram-Sin's rule, the Akkadians controlled the area from Elam in southwest Iran, Sumer, Akkad, and part of northern Syria. Most of the evidence for these borders comes from dedications with inscriptions that record the campaigns of Naram-Sin or boundary markers with his name that are set up in these regions. The expeditions were focused on controlling trade routes—for example, ensuring access to the Indus Valley and to northern Syria and from there to the Mediterranean. In Syria, at Tell Brak, bricks from a monumental building that had Naram-Sin's name stamped on them show that he sponsored the structure and that the Akkadians intended to settle there, perhaps installing a garrison of troops in this city, again to make sure that they could control the trade routes in the area.

Naram-Sin adopted a new title, we're not exactly sure when. The title is "King of the Four Corners of the World." This essentially defined him as the ruler of the known world. We've discussed the importance of titles to this point, but now we have a new one that is more descriptive of what the Akkadians actually controlled. It's no longer listing a number of cities, although those can appear in inscriptions, but instead it's controlling the entire world. One of the most significant revolts against Akkadian rule came from an alliance of southern city-states. This is unusual because it was a very strong coalition of rulers and armies from the south, and it shows unusual cooperation between those cities. It also demonstrates for us that there was widespread discontent with Akkadian rule in the south. Naram-Sin shattered this alliance—as I said, he was a very strong military leader—and after this, Naram-Sin chose a new way of describing himself and a whole new concept of rulership. He deified himself; he made himself a god for the latter part of his reign. Certainly after he defeated this coalition from the south, we know that he used the sign for a deity right before his name in all the written records. This sign is actually the symbol of a star that indicates that a god's name will follow; in this case, Naram-Sin's name will follow. This is an unprecedented act for a Mesopotamian ruler and it may have been one reason for the later hostility toward him, but it is unclear what the immediate reaction would have been. An inscription honoring Naram-Sin notes that, "when the four corners of the universe…were hostile to him, he remained victorious in nine battles in a single year because of the love that Ishtar had for him...." Remember Ishtar is the later term for Inanna. Because of Naram-Sin's success, the people of his city asked the gods, as the inscription continues, "that he be the god of their city Akkad, and they built a temple for him in the midst of Akkad."

Naram-Sin also portrayed himself in a new and radical way in the visual arts. We have the sign for a divinity before his name and we also see him portrayed in a way that is much closer to the way the gods had been portrayed. A limestone relief sculpture, about six feet tall, called the Victory Stele of Naram-Sin is now in the Louvre. It shows the king as a victor over a mountain tribe, the Lullubi in Elam. Some aspects of the image are familiar. Naram-Sin is much larger than any other figures on the stele and he is the focus of attention. He is shown at the head of his troops; he is moving up a mountainside. All of this visual imagery shows that Naram-Sin is doing what a good king was required to do.

There are several innovations, however. First, instead of the usual rows of figures that we've come very accustomed to seeing in Mesopotamian art, the entire background of this image is employed. Naram-Sin is defeating a mountain tribe, the Lullubi, and he is shown climbing up a mountain. His army follows him. In addition to the mountain, other topographical features are detailed. We see another mountain in the background, so this is clearly a mountainous region. There is also a tree, the leaves of which are detailed very specifically and scholars argue over what type of tree it is. Clearly, this is a desire on the part of the artist to display a specific battle. The usual motif of the victor crushing his enemies beneath his feet is retained, but these opponents are not nude and they wear short skirts. This could convey to the viewer that the battle is still going on. They see Naram-Sin as he is moving up the mountainside. This idea of the immediacy of the conflict is reinforced by the figure who falls in front of Naram-Sin; he is pulling an arrow out of his throat. So, Naram-Sin has not yet killed him, but we get the sense that he was the one who shot the arrow that brought this enemy down. Perhaps, it's even the king of the Lullubi.

The most important change in this representation is that Naram-Sin is shown wearing the attributes of a god and this is conveyed specifically by a horned helmet. Only the gods wore this type of helmet and the tradition had been longstanding, in use for over a thousand years. In addition, his divinity is underscored by the fact that there are no other gods shown on the stele. If you compare this to the Stele of the Vultures, which we discussed a few lectures ago, there the god of the city Ningirsu went into battle on behalf of his city. So, on one side of that stele, we saw the god and he is collecting enemies in a battle net. Fighting on the other side was the king who led his army into battle. On Naram-Sin's stele, the gods are represented symbolically by little stars that were carved at the top of the stele, so this sign that we now know accompanied Naram-Sin's name is used in the visual arts to show that the gods are present, but they are not actively involved in the battle. Instead, it is the king himself who is now divine and who now takes the battlefield on behalf of his city.

Another divine or at least a superhuman feature of Naram-Sin is the way that his body is rendered. We've seen kings before and they're somewhat block-like; they wear the long skirts and their bodies are not shown in any especially specific way. Naram-Sin wears a different costume. He wears a short skirt that falls between his legs; this may have been a battle costume. He has one sleeve, but the other arm, his right arm, is bare and the arm is shown in a very muscular and well-developed way. He's quite sexy, as one scholar has described Naram-Sin. This emphasis on his body underscores both his physical strength and also resembles the way that artists have typically shown gods or heroes. So, kings are shown in one way in earlier art, but the gods and the heroes, such as Gilgamesh, wore this type of costume when they were engaged in combat and they also had very specific renderings of their bodies. You recall that in the Epic of Gilgamesh, the poet reminded the audience frequently about how strong and how attractive and beautiful Gilgamesh was. There was this great emphasis on his physical perfection. You can see that Naram-Sin would inspire the same admiration just by looking at the way he's shown on this victory stele.

Certainly, Naram-Sin as represented on the stele in the Louvre fulfills the title of "King of the Four Corners of the World," and of a ruler who could be divine. It's hard to know how his subjects would have responded to the news that Naram-Sin had suddenly become a god. But, given his success in battle, he could very well have seemed godlike. Remember that divinities in Mesopotamia drew their power from nature and so they controlled the environment and any environmental disaster was seen as the representation of the power of the gods. If a king comes to your city and destroys its walls or attacks the population and really changes your environment, he could seem much more godlike than we might imagine him to be. So, keep that idea of Mesopotamian divinity, as well as the fact that the kings were chosen by the gods. They are already the closest humans to the gods, so this may not have seemed as great a leap in Mesopotamia as it does to us.

One theory explains Naram-Sin's divination as an attempt for the Akkadian king to break down or to at least divert the strong identification with individual cities, their ruling elite, their gods, their temples, and their history. We can see that it would be a significant drawback to a regional state or empire if a scribe in Ur saw herself first as a citizen of Ur, rather than a subject to the king of Akkad. By creating a new and successful cult to the King of the Four Corners of the World, Naram-Sin would establish a common, unifying theme throughout the lands that he governed. This is a next step from what we saw Sargon do with his daughter Enheduanna. By making her the priestess of Ur and other cults, he made sure that a member of his family was identified as a major religious leader in southern Mesopotamia. Now, Naram-Sin is taking the next step, using a new cult to try and unify this area. We don't know how successful this was; it would be fascinating to know what people actually thought when it was announced that Naram-Sin was a god. There's clear discomfort with Naram-Sin's divinity in the later sources, and they use this arrogance and sense of impiety as a way to explain the collapse of Akkadian rule. There is no evidence from sources that date to Naram-Sin's rule that there was any challenge to his identification as a god, but of course there wouldn't be. We don't ever see a written source really challenge a king, at least not up to this point.

One of the later texts, *The Curse of Akkad*, explained the fall of the Akkadians, blaming Naram-Sin specifically for his impiety and this resulted in the collapse of the Akkadian Dynasty. The inscription is supposedly a copy from a stele set up by Naram-Sin. Enlil visited Naram-Sin in a dream in which the god revealed a terrifying future for Akkad. Naram-Sin refused to share this dream with anyone, but instead hid in his palace for several years—for seven years, in fact. At the end of that time, he attacked the temple of Enlil at Nippur. Remember how important Nippur was as a religious center in southern Mesopotamia. That is where all of the kings were given their authority, were given their symbolic approval of Enlil, the king of the gods for their reign. *The Curse of Akkad* writes that:

> Like a robber plundering the city, he set tall ladders against the temple. To demolish E-Kur as if it were a huge ship, to break up its soil like the soil of mountains where precious metals are mined, to splinter it like the lapis lazuli mountains…he had large axes cast, he had double-edged axes sharpened to be used against it.

The E-Kur is the temple of Enlil at Nippur. The text goes on: "With the possessions being taken away from the city, good sense left Akkad."

Enlil's rage, as recorded in *The Curse of Akkad*, is intense and he sent a mountain tribe, "the Gutians, an unbridled people, with human intelligence but canine instincts and monkey features. Like small birds they swooped on the ground in great flocks…nothing escaped their clutches, no one left their grasp. Messengers no longer traveled the highways…brigands occupied the highways. The doors of the city gates of the land lay dislodged in the mud…" The motif of foreign tribes acting as the agents of the gods was a common explanation for a change in power in Mesopotamian literature. These foreign tribes often don't live in cities, but rather in the mountains or even in the deserts where cities wouldn't really be possible because they didn't have access to the water that was necessary. You remember that we discussed the idea that geography would promote smaller communities that were less integrated with each other. And, the invading tribes that are described in these texts always are very foreign, very remote, and not connected to the rest of the area that they are attacking.

The texts also characterize these invading tribes—in this particular case, the Gutians—as uncivilized, which would probably make them especially fearsome. When the Mesopotamians would combine their lack of civilization with their animal-like appearance, which often occurs in these texts, they would seem completely savage. It's really hard not to imagine the Gutians as the flying monkeys from *The Wizard of Oz*; all my students immediately think of that image when I have them read this text. All of the phrases used to describe the Gutians separated them from the normal daily life of Mesopotamia. If we compare these written descriptions with the visual representations of enemies, we thought about why Mesopotamian artists would want to show the enemy nude with their hands behind their backs, and this is a similar way to dehumanize one's opponents in both visual and written texts.

The Akkadian Empire would last for at least another 20 years after the death of Naram-Sin, and this belies the swift image of divine retribution against Naram-Sin given in the texts. There's very little archaeological evidence for destruction or major disruptions in the cities at this time. Nothing has been found archaeologically that would confirm what is described in *The Curse of Akkad* and we have to be satisfied with suggestions of rebellion in the written text, rather than this complete destruction in the region.

Sharkali-Sharri, the king of Akkad who succeeded Naram-Sin and ruled from 2217–2193 B.C., gave up the title of King of the Four Corners of the World during his reign. This is significant; it indicates a general withdrawal of the kingdom of Akkad to the north, abandoning the south. The Gutians returned and they were much more successful in these invasions after Naram-Sin's rule than during it. They briefly controlled southern Mesopotamia. Sharkali-Sharri's reign seems to have been largely concerned with defense against both internal and external threats—the Gutians, as well as internal disruption within the kingdom of Akkad. For a couple of years after Sharkali-Sharri's reign, there was no leader; there was no king. The Sumerian king list records in this memorable phrase, "Who was king? Who was not king?" If we think about how focused the Sumerian king list on showing the continuous holding of the office of kingship, this concession to the chaos of the era is really significant and shows that there was no one who could control the region. It seems wild and unruly.

In Mesopotamia, this was a period in which the city-states regained their autonomy from Akkadian control and no single power controlled more than one city in the region. After the fall of the Akkadians, I will now refer to central and southern Mesopotamia as Babylonia to reflect the fact that there is a consistent political unit— and that is the city-state—and that there's also religious, linguistic, and cultural accord in the region. Babylonia will continue as an identifiable and distinct region almost until the end of the course.

One example of a newly independent city-state that emerged after the Akkadians fell is Lagash in Sumer. Lagash benefited from the disruption at the end of the Akkadian period and by the late 3rd millennium had reestablished self-rule. The details of this process really can't be sorted out until we come to the reign of Gudea. Gudea was the second ruler of the dynasty that took control of Lagash and he is one of the best-known rulers of the era not because of his accomplishments, but because of the numerous portrait sculptures that have been recovered by archaeologists. It shows that the more evidence that is recovered by archaeologists, the more attention you get. Gudea is not especially noteworthy and the chance discovery of several statues of the king make him one of the most recognizable rulers in Mesopotamian history.

The statues of Gudea emphasize the ruler's piety and humility before the gods, so it's a distinct change from Naram-Sin's way of representing himself. The ruler clasps his hands in the position familiar from earlier Mesopotamian votive sculpture. In contrast to his bearded, longhaired Akkadian predecessors, Gudea is smooth-shaven and his hair is short or tucked up beneath a cap; sometimes we can't quite tell. This hairstyle is much more closely allied with the way that priests showed themselves than with the way the Akkadian rulers presented themselves. Even though Gudea rejected much of the visual iconography that Naram-Sin used, he did retain the focus on his physical strength that Naram-Sin displays. Most statues that survive show very well developed biceps; even though he's pious, he's still sexy. Certain sculptures also depict Gudea engaged in building temples and even show an architectural plan of a temple that he sponsored. So, he is reverting to traditional concerns of rulers.

These images reinforce his close involvement in and concern for projects that kings had traditionally been focused on, and it returns to a much different way of ruling than the Akkadian kings had chosen. It was an era in which there was a significant amount of political fragmentation and change, and it would be useful for a king such as Gudea to keep his attention on local needs. It probably also reflects localization and fragmentation of the economy. There may have been a shift back to a focus on agriculture as the main base of the economy, rather than the trade routes that the Akkadian rulers were so focused on controlling. It's hard to piece that type of information together, but there is a definite focus on the city-state and a focus on what kings have been doing for millennia in Gudea's rule. He is the ruler that we know best from southern Mesopotamia and from this period. We have to extrapolate from these images, to imagine that in other cities the kings would undertake the same type of local focus. If the tribes that had threatened the Akkadians—the Gutians or even other threats from neighbors to the south or even to the west—if that continued in the absence of a strong central government and especially a strong military focus that the Akkadians had, the standing army that Sargon controlled, then it may have been difficult for city-states to engage in the type of long-distance trade that the Akkadians had tried to establish. That, too, could emphasize the importance of the city-state and take the rulers back to local issues and local politics, as it were.

The sculpted portraits that we have discussed illustrate the very different ways that these two rulers—Naram-Sin and Gudea—presented themselves and they reflect the broader message to their people. They also provide a sort of visual bookend for the history of this period. Naram-Sin proclaims himself a god both in his texts and in his artistic representations. He did this for very specific reasons that would reinforce his political control of a large territory. So, he is trying to establish himself as a god of a large area, rather than the god of a specific city-state, such as Akkad, who happens to establish political control. This may have seemed very radical at the time, but it is going to be adopted by the next great dynasty that we will meet, the Ur III rulers, who even though they do present themselves as gods, they take a slightly different tone than Naram-Sin does in their visual representations and also in their written sources for the era.

Lecture Sixteen
The Ur III Dynasty

Scope:

In the last lecture, we discussed the end of Akkadian control of northern and southern Mesopotamia. Later authors excoriated Naram-Sin, the grandson of Sargon of Akkad, for his supposed impiety, which they blamed for the fall of Akkad. Contemporary sources for Naram-Sin's rule reveal a different story: He ruled for more than 30 years, and it was not until the reign of his successors that the city-states of Mesopotamia revolted against Akkadian control. One of those newly independent city-states was Ur, which soon dominated Babylonia. During their hegemony, the rulers of the Ur III dynasty (c. 2112–2004 B.C.) organized a much more centralized government that effectively controlled the region for more than 100 years. In this lecture, we meet the ruler Shulgi, whose reign represents a high point in the prosperity and art of the Ur III period. He established a system of taxation and is credited as the author of the oldest surviving law code. For Shulgi's successors, the prosperity of the Ur III era came to a sudden halt with a period of economic instability and attacks from foreign invaders, the Amorites from the west and the Elamites from the east.

Outline

I. A hallmark of the Ur III period is the overwhelming number of texts that document its political and economic history. More than 40,000 texts have been translated, and thousands more remain to be published and analyzed.

   A. These texts are largely economic, primarily official state records and receipts; few private trade or other transactions are noted.

   B. Further, historical records or accounts of military campaigns are rare, which means that details not relating to civil government can be difficult to sort out.

II. The era we are discussing is called the Ur III period or dynasty because, according to the Sumerian king list, it encompasses the third group of rulers from Ur to hold kingship.

A. Ur-Nammu (r. c. 2112–2094 B.C.) was the first of five kings of the Ur III dynasty. He took the title "King of Sumer and Akkad," indicating that he held regional control. Ur-Nammu ruled over Babylonia and the lands to the east along the Zagros Mountains.

B. Ur-Nammu promoted the traditional religious preeminence of Ur through numerous building projects, including ziggurats at Ur, Uruk, Nippur, and Eridu. His name is inscribed on the mudbricks used to build these structures.

    1. The ziggurat at Ur is one of the best preserved of this type of structure. It was placed in a walled-off precinct that itself was raised on a platform. Two of three stories of the ziggurat are preserved; they now stand about 60 feet high, on a foundation measuring 200 by 150 feet.

    2. Three long stairways on the northeast side, one in the center and one on each side, provide access to a landing between the first and second levels; the central staircase would have continued to the top level.

C. Written and archaeological evidence for Ur-Nammu's reign describes his attention to rebuilding and restoring temples and his work reopening trade. Given his religious activities, it comes as something of a surprise to learn that Ur-Nammu died in battle, which was quite rare for a king.

III. The most complete evidence we have for the Ur III period comes from the long reign of Ur-Nammu's son, Shulgi (r. c. 2094–2047 B.C.).

A. A number of sources testify to Shulgi's success and allow us to trace major events in his reign.

B. The earliest collection of royal laws is attributed to either Shulgi or to his father, Ur-Nammu. The laws show the involvement of the king in ensuring justice for his people, a concept that we will discuss in more detail in connection with Hammurabi in Lecture Twenty-One.

C. Diplomatic negotiations, specifically marriage with the families of powerful neighboring states, increased the size and prosperity of the Ur III kingdom. Shulgi himself had nine wives, including a princess from Mari, the wealthy trading center on the northern Euphrates River.

D. One of the most important domestic reforms enacted by Shulgi was the creation of an elaborate unified bureaucracy that joined southern and northern Babylonia. This bureaucracy is known from the extensive record-keeping that preserves a standardized system of weights and measures, a new calendar, and the administrative and military hierarchy of the court.

1. Shulgi was active in restructuring the administration of his kingdom. In the heartland of the Ur III kingdom, he created about 20 provinces, each governed by an *ensi* who usually belonged to the local elite.

2. The palace also sent a military commander, or *shagina*, to the provinces, who reported directly to the palace. A *shagina* was often related to the royal family and, presumably, was more loyal to the king than a local *ensi* might be.

E. Shulgi established two new systems for taxing his kingdom, both drawing on the concept of the *bala* tax. *Bala* is the Sumerian word for "exchange."

1. Cities closest to Ur were required to provide local goods to the palace.

2. Provinces located farther away from Ur were compelled to send cattle or sheep as tribute. These would be sent to a collection center at Puzrish-Dagan, near Nippur, then distributed to feed the palace, as sacrifices in the temples, or to other provinces.

3. One annual report records that 350,000 sheep and 28,000 cattle passed through Puzrish-Dagan during that year.

F. This state bureaucracy required a detailed system of accounting, and during this time, scribal schools adopted a new curriculum that taught the accounting system and new methods of writing on tablets.

1. Shulgi's extensive bureaucracy also supplies us with our earliest information about the education of scribes.

2. Both private and official scribal schools, called *edubba*, or "tablet houses," existed.

3. A scribe would begin his or her education at a young age, perhaps as early as seven years old. It would have

taken many years to learn the vast number of signs necessary to gain employment as a scribe.

4. In addition to the cuneiform signs, scribes would also need to be familiar with methods of accounting for rations, labor, and other necessities in order to document the economic aspects of the palace or temple or private transactions.

5. Scribes were compensated with rations, textiles, beer, or land. We see evidence for scribes at all economic levels, some very wealthy, others earning a more modest living.

IV. Shulgi made himself a god about halfway through his reign and set a precedent for his successors in the Ur III dynasty to be worshipped as gods.

A. As we saw with the Akkadian king Naram-Sin, this self-deification may have been an attempt to weaken ties to the city-state and strengthen the connection to the central government.

B. *Praise poems*, often called hymns by modern translators, describe the prowess of the king in every aspect of his rule. These are written in the first person from the point of view of the king himself.

1. Shulgi's praise poems celebrate his preeminence among rulers, as well as his divine heritage, with long descriptions of his strength and intellectual qualities. Shulgi is also described as one of the few literate rulers.

2. Kings often relied on priests or diviners to reveal the meaning of signs in dreams or animal organs, but in his praise poems, Shulgi performed this difficult task for his diviner.

3. Praise poems also report the duties of the king, indicating that a king had to demonstrate his skills and interest in the well-being of his people and had to make his mastery of the land explicit.

V. Shulgi's reign was the high point of the Ur III period.

A. A combination of internal economic disruption and threats from the borders led to the end of the Ur III era during the reign of the last member of the dynasty, Ibbi-Sin (r. c. 2028–2004 B.C.).

B. Shulgi's son Shu-Sin (r. c. 2037–2029 B.C.) built a defensive wall along the northern border of his land, but this proved ineffective protection against incursions from the Amorites.

C. Other pressures from Elam further weakened the state and placed demands on its limited resources.

    1. One of the important domestic problems was the end of the *bala* tax system and the failure of the central government to collect tribute.

    2. Collection of the *bala* tax stopped in the ninth year of Ibbi-Sin's rule, which suggests that provincial ties to the throne were weakening. Texts also report a famine and an increase in grain prices at about this time.

D. One of Ibbi-Sin's former generals, Ishbi-Erra, took control of the city of Isin and set up a rival dynasty there.

    1. Texts, as usual, blame foreigners, in this case, the Amorites from the western desert, for disrupting the rule of the Ur III kings.

    2. As most of the cities in his kingdom defected to local rulers or other leaders, Ibbi-Sin retreated to Ur. After a long siege, the Elamites captured Ibbi-Sin and destroyed the city of Ur.

E. Although later kings rarely mention the Ur III rulers, the large number of surviving texts allows us to the see the brief prosperity of this era.

F. With the end of the Ur III dynasty about 2000 B.C., we enter a period in which city-states reemerge as independent from central control.

Essential Reading:

Jacob Klein, "Shulgi of Ur: King of a Neo-Sumerian Empire," in *CANE*, vol. II, pp. 843–858.

Graham Cunningham, et al., *The Literature of Ancient Sumer*, pp. 304–307.

Supplementary Reading:

Marc Van De Mieroop, *A History of the Ancient Near East, ca. 3000–323 BC*, pp. 69–79.

Questions to Consider:

1. Is it possible to identify any aspects of Akkadian rule adopted in the Ur III dynasty?

2. How does the praise poem of Shulgi celebrate his achievements?

Lecture Sixteen—Transcript
The Ur III Dynasty

In the last lecture, we discussed the end of Akkadian control of northern and southern Mesopotamia. Later authors excoriated Naram-Sin, the grandson of Sargon of Akkad, for his supposed impiety, which they blamed for the fall of Akkad. Contemporary sources for Naram-Sin's rule reveal a different story; Naram-Sin ruled for over 40 years and it was not until the reign of his successors that the city-states of Mesopotamia revolted against Akkadian control and gained their own independence. It's important to keep in mind the model that the Akkadian Dynasty set for later Mesopotamian rulers.

Akkad was the first city-state that expanded its control far beyond the area of its origin in northern Mesopotamia to the south. No other king before Sargon had ever traveled as far, taken his armies on such exotic expeditions, and been so successful. Naram-Sin also was successful militarily. So, it's important to know that one of the reasons why Sargon and Naram-Sin became so legendary and so important in later sources is that they established this new way of thinking about kingship and empire.

One of those newly independent city-states was Ur, which soon dominated Babylonia. During their hegemony, the rulers of the Ur III Dynasty organized a much more centralized government that effectively controlled the region for over a hundred years. This contrast with the Akkadian Dynasty in previous years because even though they had a strong military, we saw that it was very difficult for them to control the region closely and monitor activities. A hallmark of the Ur III period is the overwhelming number of texts that document its political and, even more important, its economic history. Over 40,000 texts have been translated and thousands more, perhaps even another 30,000 or 40,000 must still be published and analyzed. One of the challenges for scholars is to evaluate this huge mass of material. It can be very exciting to get so many details, but they have to be evaluated in order to get a sense of the overall structure of the Ur III society. You should be saying by now that I'm never happy; I either have too few texts or too many, and that is the constant challenge for scholars to try and reconstruct events. The texts from Ur III are largely economic and almost all are official state receipts and records; very few private trade or other transactions are noted. So, it's very much as if we try to reconstruct American history by looking only at tax returns and you can see the challenges and the emphasis on specific elements of society that would result from such sources. Another caveat about this period is that few historical records that would document military campaigns, for example, survive. So, details other than civil government can be difficult to sort out.

Ur-Nammu was the first of five kings of the Ur III dynasty. It's called the Ur III Dynasty or period because, according to the Sumerian king list, it is the third time that a group of rulers from the city of Ur held kingship. You haven't missed the first two; I just haven't discussed them in very much detail. Ur-Nammu took the title of King of Sumer and Akkad and this shows that this phrase now indicates regional control. He's picking up on what Sargon first created. Ur-Nammu ruled over Babylonia and the lands to the east along the Zagros Mountains.

One of the activities that Ur-Nammu is best known for is his promotion of the traditional religious preeminence of Ur through numerous building projects, including ziggurats at Ur, Uruk, Nippur, and Eridu. This shows us how important his regional control was and also that he used the rebuilding or construction of temples as a way to consolidate his power. We know that Ur-Nammu was responsible for these ziggurats because his name is inscribed on the mudbricks that were used to construct them. The ziggurat at Ur is one of the best preserved of this type of structure. If you remember when Leonard Woolley excavated at Ur, it was because the ziggurat was still visible in the area. The ziggurat was placed in a walled-off structure, which itself was raised on a platform. So, the entire temple precinct is above the rest of the city. Two of three stories of the ziggurat are preserved and they now stand about 60 feet high, on a foundation that spreads about 200 by 150 feet. There are three long stairways on the northeast side of the ziggurat—one in the center and one on each side—and these provide access to a landing between the first and second levels of the ziggurat. The central staircase would have continued up to the top level, giving access to the shrine that would have originally stood at the top of the ziggurat. If you see a reconstruction of a ziggurat, it probably draws on Ur-Nammu's ziggurat at Ur for its model, so you will become quite familiar with Ur-Nammu's ziggurat.

Both the written and archaeological evidence for Ur-Nammu's reign describe his attention to rebuilding and restoring temples and also to his work freeing his people from "thieves, robbers, and rebels." These would have been the invaders that came from different parts of the borders of Mesopotamia and he had to reopen the highways to make them safe for his people to travel, and also to restore the trade that was so important to the Mesopotamian economy. It comes as something of a surprise with all of this focus on Ur-Nammu's religious activity that we learn that he died in battle. An inscription records that he was "abandoned on the battlefield like a smashed vessel." It is very rare for a Mesopotamian ruler to die in battle, so when it happens both the sources note it usually as a way to describe punishment for some impious action that he's taken. That's not the case for Ur-Nammu, but it does cause quite a bit of concern for his successors and for his people to learn that a king could die in battle.

We have the most complete evidence for the Ur III period during the long reign of Ur-Nammu's son Shulgi, who ruled from 2094–2047 B.C. A number of sources attest to Shulgi's success and allow us to trace the major events in his reign, mostly in the area of his governance and bureaucratic control of Babylonia. The earliest collection of royal laws—just a few fragments—is attributed to either Shulgi or his father, Ur-Nammu. These laws show the involvement of the king in ensuring justice for his people and we'll come to this concept in a later lecture when we discuss the law code of Hammurabi. Diplomatic negotiations, specifically marriage with families of powerful neighboring states are attested for the Ur III period. These would increase both the size and prosperity of the kingdom. Shulgi himself had nine wives, including a princess from Mari, the wealthy trading center on the northern Euphrates River. If you recall, the Akkadian kings, Sargon and Naram-Sin, attacked these cities as a way to control them. Shulgi now returns to a more diplomatic alliance with the region, probably because it was so difficult to control an area far from the heartland of his kingdom.

One of the most important domestic reforms enacted by Shulgi was the creation of an elaborate, unified bureaucracy that joined southern and northern Babylonia. This bureaucracy is known from the extensive record keeping that preserves a standardized system of weights and measures, a new calendar, and the administrative and military hierarchy of the court. Shulgi was active in restructuring the administration of his kingdom. In the heartland of the Ur III kingdom, he created about 20 provinces, each governed by an *ensi*, who usually belonged to the local elite. This is a pattern that we'll see later rulers draw on. They would alternate between promoting someone who was familiar with the area and who had been important in the city in previous years, requiring them to be loyal to the state. But, often, the drawback to this is that the local ruler will then decide that he should rebel from his overlord. This will happen at the end of the Ur III period, but we'll see Mesopotamian kings alternate between drawing on the local elite to help them govern or installing members of their family or someone whom they think is more loyal to them. Shulgi combined these two ideas by sending a military commander or shagina to report directly to the palace and this would be someone whom Shulgi felt very comfortable with and knew that they would be loyal to them. Often, a shagina was related to the royal family—with nine wives, that was not difficult—and, presumably, this would make him more loyal to the king than a local *ensi* would be. So, Shulgi tries to use both models, but we'll see it doesn't quite work.

Shulgi also established a new way of taxing his kingdom and he used two different systems. Both drew on the concept of a bala tax. A bala is the Sumerian word for exchange and this was a method of tribute that exchanged goods that were produced locally for what the palace wanted. Those cities closest to Ur would provide goods that they had produced locally. This would allow Shulgi to compel a higher tribute because he knew the productivity of the area was very high. For example, a city that was very focused on growing grain, an agricultural based economy, would have to provide grain to the court. Whereas another city that had a wider manufacturing economy, such as leather making or furniture making or reed weaving, they would send those types of goods to the king as part of their tribute. Farther away from southern Mesopotamia, provinces would send sheep or goats or other types of animals as tribute to the king. These were sent to a site called Puzrish-Dagan, which was near Nippur. Then, they would be redistributed to feed the palace. They would be used as sacrifices in the temples. They may even be sent to other provinces that required cattle or sheep or some other type of meat product or wool, in the case of sheep. The palace would oversee this entire redistribution. So, we get back to an idea that we saw early on with the temple as a redistributive center that would collect excess goods and then send them where they were necessary. Now the court does this, the king oversees this, and some of these records have survived. So, we know what goods were collected, how many were collected, and we get a sense of an enormous scale that the Ur III kings controlled.

One annual report records that 350,000 sheep and 28,000 cattle passed through Puzrish-Dagan during that single year. That gives you some sense of the amount of tribute that was being sent to collection centers and then could be redistributed throughout the kingdom. This state bureaucracy required a detailed system of accounting and during this time scribal schools adopted a new curriculum that allowed them to learn the new accounting system; remember I said Shulgi instituted a new system of weights and measurements, so they had to learn how to use this method. It also was a period when there was a shift in the way that cuneiform texts were actually written on the tablets. The shift was from a sort of vertical way of dividing the tablets to a horizontal way. These innovations in record keeping are one reason why we have so much evidence for this period, because a lot of texts from earlier periods had to be rewritten and so they are stored in these areas.

Shulgi's extensive bureaucracy also supplies us with our earliest information about the education of scribes. Both private and official scribal schools, which are called *edubba* or tablet houses, existed. We learn that a scribe would begin his education at a young age, perhaps as early as seven years old. Both male and female scribes are recorded, although it's fairly rare for a female name to appear in these records, but they do exist. It would take several years to learn the vast number of signs that would be necessary to gain employment, especially employment for the crown, for the king. In addition to the cuneiform signs, scribes would also have to be familiar with the new accounting methods that would be used to record rations, labor, and any other necessity that records economic aspects of the palace, in some instances a temple or in rare cases for the Ur IIII period, even private transactions. Scribes were compensated with rations, textiles, beer, or even land. We see evidence for scribes at all economic levels; some are very wealthy and those would be the scribes who worked for the king. Others earned a much more modest living, sort of scratching out some way of supporting themselves. These would be scribes that recorded individual transactions, so they couldn't count on a steady income necessarily.

Shulgi, much like our Akkadian predecessor Naram-Sin, made himself a god about halfway through his reign and this set a precedent in the Ur III dynasty for kings to be worshipped as gods. As with Naram-Sin, this may have been an attempt to weaken the city-state and to strengthen the connection to the central government. We have no later sources that condemn Shulgi as they did Naram-Sin, so the idea of the king as a god seems to have been very well accepted by this point. Shulgi also took the title, King of the Four Corners of the World, which Naram-Sin had created. It's a return to a broader sense of scale and power that these later rulers took from their Akkadian predecessors.

Praise poems, often called hymns by modern translators, described the prowess of the king in every aspect of his rule and these are much more detailed than our earlier inscriptions that might focus on military success, usually some sense of dominance. But, Shulgi's praise poems or hymns are quite detailed and long, and they celebrate his preeminence among rulers, as well as his divine heritage. There are long descriptions of his physical strength and his intellectual qualities. In one poem, Shulgi writes about how quickly he can run. He's not just fast, but he has a lot of endurance, so he describes himself as a donkey. All of these praise poems are written in the first-person, so it creates a sense to the modern way of looking at political readers, that we have a very arrogant king. But, we should probably think of him as enthusiastic and trying to show every area that he succeeds in and this would be comforting to his people. They would know that he was not just physically strong, but he was also smart.

Shulgi is one of the very few literate rulers that we know of. Most kings probably did not bother to learn to read or write because they would have a whole force of scribes to do that for them. Shulgi writes in one of these poems: "When I was small, I was at the academy, where I learned the scribal art from the tablets of Sumer and Akkad." So, he learned both Sumerian and Akkadian. "None of the nobles could write on clay as I could. I qualified fully in subtraction, addition, reckoning, and accounting." Here we see that he is literate and he has learned all of the math skills necessary, which would be a very useful skill for a ruler.

Kings often relied on priests or diviners to reveal the meaning of signs; we've seen dreams. But, there's also a method of divine correspondence with humans that is the study of animal organs—extispicy. The only way to really explain this is to keep in mind that all of nature is divine and so, if you look at the liver of a sheep, of course the gods would have sent some message to be written on this liver. It's probably one of the most difficult religious concepts to reconcile today. Shulgi performed this difficult task himself. He writes: "Then, as I prepare the sheep with words of prayer, my diviner watches in amazement like an idiot. The prepared sheep is placed at my disposal, and I never confuse a favorable sign with an unfavorable one. I myself have a clear intuition, and I judge by my own eyes. In the insides of just one sheep I, the king, can find the indications for everything and everywhere." So, he has complete control of everything he needs as king. He doesn't need to rely on his servants or other members of his court.

He continues that he's not just someone who is focused on the specific duties of mathematics and divination; he also is a musician. "I, Shulgi, king of Ur, have also devoted myself to the art of music. Nothing is too complicated for me; I know…the perfection of the art of music…" We've seen the lyres from the royal cemetery at Ur, and kings may very well have participated in religious festivals and sung hymns to the gods themselves. So, this too is an intellectual accomplishment of Shulgi and it's one that is worthy of note for his subjects. The hymn closes with a summary of his skills:

> Until the distant future may this song bless the name of me, the king, with a life of long days…With the awesomeness that radiates from my forehead, which I make the foreign lands wear like a nose-rope, and the fear-inspiring luster…I am able to root out and undo crime. I have the ability to reconcile great matters with one word.

So, he is also a diplomat, a judge, and he is concerned for the justice and crime that his people have to endure.

These praise poems give us a very good indication of the duties of the king and the details indicate that a king had to demonstrate his skills. His interest in the well-being of his people had to be repeated again and again to show that he really was concerned for them. He had to make the mastery of his land and everything needed to govern it quite explicit. Shulgi's one of my very favorite rulers. If you're having a bad day, you can read about all of the great qualities that Shulgi has.

Shulgi's reign was the high point of the Ur III period. Since it's also the best documented, it receives the most attention from scholars. After his reign, a combination of internal economic disruption and threats from the borders would result in the end of the Ur III era during the reign of the last member of the Ur III Dynasty, Ibbi-Sin, who ruled from 2028–2004 B.C. Shulgi's son, Shu-Sin, who ruled from 2037–2029 B.C., had built a defensive wall that was over 150 miles long along the northern border of his land. This was supposed to provide some protection from the incursions of a nomadic group called the Amorites, and we will meet the Amorites again so remember that we see them first here. We know that in addition to this pressure from the north, the culture of Elam to the south further weakened the state and created demands on its limited resources.

One of the important domestic problems was the end of the bala tax system and the failure of the central government to collect tribute. This meant that it did not have the vast treasury that it had originally compelled from its provinces. It also meant that the king could not provide the necessities and the resources that he had been able to earlier, so this would have weakened loyalty to the Ur III kings. We know that collection of the bala tax stopped in the ninth year of Ibbi-Sin's rule, and this shows us that the central government was unable to exert control over its provinces. We also learn from surviving texts that there was a famine and huge inflation in grain prices at about this time. There's a text from Ibbi-Sin to one of his former generals asking him—begging him, really—to send grain. This general, this shagina, Ishbi-Erra, shows the difficulty in maintaining loyalty to a ruler. He had set up control of the city of Nippur and established a new rival dynasty there that would challenge, quite successfully, the Ur III kings.

Later texts, as usual, blame foreigners—in this case, the Amorites from the western desert—for disrupting the rule of the Ur III kings. What's also interesting about these later sources and the way that they describe the end of the Ur III period is that there is a lack of surprise. For one of the few times in Mesopotamian history, the end of a dynasty or the end of a kingdom, is not blamed on the impiety of a ruler. But, when the Ur III period is described later on, it's simply credited that it came to the end of its era. Its time for control of kingship was ended. We see, archaeologically, that there is other evidence for the disruption at the end of the Ur III period. As cities in the kingdom defected to local rulers or other leaders, Ibbi-Sin retreated back to the city of Ur and fortified it with large walls, which are documented in the archaeological record. After a long siege, the Elamites captured Ibbi-Sin and destroyed the city of Ur; they took him back to Elam as a prisoner. While later kings rarely mention the Ur III rulers in contrast to the Akkadian kings, the large number of surviving texts allows us to see the prosperity, however brief, of this era. It also means that scholars are very focused on the Ur III period because we have evidence for it, so it can often receive more attention in histories than other periods that we are less well informed about.

With the end of the Ur III dynasty at about 2000 B.C., we will enter a period in which many city-states reemerge as independent from any central control. Certain successful military leaders could control a larger territory around the city-state for a brief time, but no single city or ruler united northern and southern Mesopotamia under his rule until Hammurabi of Babylon who ruled from 1792–1750. In the next lecture, we will depart from our study of the political history and go back to examine the society and, specifically, what cities look like in this period when they are so important; we will return to the theme of urbanism.

Lecture Seventeen
Life in a Mesopotamian City

Scope:

In this lecture, we will return to one of the themes of our course, urbanism, to trace the developments that have occurred since the Uruk era. We know the importance of the major public institutions, particularly temples, in cities, and we know that palaces supported large workforces. What can we reconstruct about the rest of the city? Keep in mind that the archaeological evidence is richest for temples and palaces, so that what survives for the rest of the city is quite scattered. We will extrapolate from several centuries and many different sites to create a picture of urban life. As we will see, texts fill in some important gaps, but many questions remain. We will begin on a small scale, with an average house and its occupants, then move on to local government, although this is an especially vague aspect of urban life. We will also discuss different professions, then close with two studies of specific cities, Sippar and Nuzi.

Outline

I. Cities can be understood as large versions of individual households; thus, any study of individual houses, both the occupants and the structure itself, is important for our understanding of the city as a whole.

   A. Fathers were the undisputed heads of the household and were surrounded by their families. Parents, sons, their wives and children, and any unmarried daughters lived together in a house.

   B. Fathers arranged the marriages of both sons and daughters. Women married in their late teens; men, in their late 20s.

   1. The groom's family would give a gift to the family of the bride; in the Early Dynastic era, this consisted of quantities of food, but later, by the 18th century B.C., the gift was silver in an amount equal to the dowry given to the groom by the bride's father.

   2. The dowry was to meant support the wife and, in the case of divorce, would be returned to the bride's family.

3. It was customary to take only one wife, unless she was unable to have children, in which case, the husband could take a second wife, although he could also adopt a child, perhaps a relative.

C. Slaves were an accepted part of Mesopotamian life; they were acquired in many ways, as prisoners of war, for example, or as infants bought from parents in periods of financial crisis.

1. Most of those who entered the condition of slavery did so to pay off a debt for themselves or a family member.

2. Theoretically, this debt slavery could be temporary, but it was difficult to earn one's freedom.

D. This multigenerational household resulted in flexible house plans, with rooms added when necessary or affordable.

E. Houses were built around open courtyards, which would provide light and air. The purpose of rooms, whether they were used for living or storage, cannot usually be identified because houses were cleared out when they were sold or rebuilt. Two exceptions to this general rule are rooms used for weaving and kitchens.

1. Weaving usually occurred in the courtyard of the house, where archaeologists often find evidence for textile manufacture in the form of loom weights and other tools necessary for weaving.

2. The location of the kitchen in a house can usually be determined because the earth there is blackened by fire.

F. Houses could be owned or rented. A surviving rental agreement of the 5th century B.C. notes that the tenant is also a builder; he receives a reduced rent in exchange for repairs made to the building.

II. Turning to local government, we find that the titles of many different local officials are preserved, but it can be challenging to understand their specific responsibilities.

A. The mayor was the leader of the court and often appeared as a witness in lawsuits. He is frequently listed as responsible for prosecuting theft.

1. One text states that the mayor was a middleman, collecting taxes from his people and sending them to some other authority.
2. The mayor would also have delivered the manpower necessary for building projects or military service required by the king.
3. The story of a poor man from Nippur reports an interaction between a mayor and one of his less prosperous citizens; the mayor comes off poorly in this tale, as politicians often do in satirical literature.
4. Mayors should probably be thought of as the representatives of the city to the palace and vice versa.

B. In addition to a mayor, each city had one or more assemblies. The chief responsibility of the leader of the assembly was to imprison people.

C. Scattered sources reveal that cities were divided into quarters or neighborhoods; at this level, leaders probably also oversaw the more mundane needs of the city.

D. The many recorded titles of officials lead us to believe that thriving urban bureaucracies were in place, but these titles don't clarify how a city actually ran.

III. Texts record a multitude of professions in urban settings.

A. Some of these ways of making a living were seasonal.

B. The food industry required bakers, butchers, gardeners, brewers, tavern-keepers, and servers.

C. Architects, draftsmen, masons, and carpenters built homes and other structures; wreckers tore down old structures to make way for new ones.

D. Boat-makers created river-craft; sailors helped merchants ply their trade; and foresters and wood collectors supplied timber for vessels.

E. Gate-keepers controlled access to the city, temple, or palace.

F. Artisans, such as basket-makers, leatherworkers, furniture-makers, or seal-cutters, produced crafts for private citizens or the palace.

1. Certain quarters of the city devoted to craft production can be identified in the archaeological record.

2. Crafts that were especially disruptive, such as tanning, or had specific technical requirements, such as kilns to fire pottery, could be placed outside the city walls or in restricted sections of the city.

G. One profession that we would expect to leave physical evidence is that of a scribe. At Nippur, a home has been identified that seems to have been the site of a small scribal school.

H. Centralized craft production is best known from the Ur III period, when the administrative documents are plentiful.

1. In this period, 13,200 weavers were employed by the palace at Ur, most of whom were women who would bring their children to the palace while they worked.

2. Weaving was a time-consuming process, requiring about 400 hours to create a garment weighing approximately seven pounds.

IV. We now turn to two examples of 2nd-millennium cities, Sippar and Nuzi.

A. At Sippar, in central Mesopotamia, the discovery of different groups of tablets has yielded valuable information about family histories and professions. One home, belonging to Ur-Utu (chief singer of lamentations of the goddess Annunitum), contained more than 2,000 tablets.

1. Many of these are devoted to real estate transactions and show that Ur-Utu owned extensive property in the area.

2. Ur-Utu's father, from whom he had inherited the house, also kept copies of numerous contracts for agricultural labor.

3. The area where these tablets were found shows some evidence of disruption, but the tablets are valuable both for the information they provide and because we know the context in which they were discovered.

B. Nuzi, near Kirkuk in northeastern Iraq, was really more of a large village than a city. Nuzi lies in the foothills of the Zagros Mountains, with Assyria to the west and Babylonia to the south.

1. Archaeologists have found nothing especially noteworthy about the economy of Nuzi, but the site

gives us a good idea of what life was like in an average small town.

2. The site dates to roughly the second half of the 2nd millennium; it is in the heartland of Assyrian territory, but at this time, Assyria was not dominant. Its population is estimated to be about 1,600 at a time when Uruk had at least 40,000 (c. 3000 B.C.).

3. The city had two large public complexes and three large suburban villas beyond the walls.

4. A drainage system of terracotta pipes removed rainwater and waste from buildings to streets or to larger drains. Manholes allowed the sewers to be cleared; waste was directed away from the city.

C. The largest building in Nuzi was the administrative center; this was not a palace but probably the site where the assembly met and the mayor conducted business. This building measures approximately 130 by 85 yards and held more than 100 rooms and storage chambers.

1. Many texts were discovered in the business section of this center, offering information about Nuzi's economy.

2. The courtyards were highly decorated and could have accommodated most of the population.

3. Living space and a small chapel have also been identified in this building.

D. The private buildings in Nuzi display a wide variety of house plans.

E. Texts from Nuzi are exceptionally informative about women's economic status.

1. We see that a woman could own real estate in her own name; in fact, we have examples of this in both small single lots and larger urban complexes.

2. Women sued and were sued in civil cases over land and in criminal cases concerning property.

3. It is significant that women were able to own property because according to all the written sources, this was the key to real wealth.

4. We also find evidence of women negotiating marriages for their children.

5. At Nuzi, women seem to have had legal parity with men; women could be witnesses in court and were treated in the same way as men, although they could not be judges. We also find parity with respect to inheritance.

6. On the whole, however, far fewer women than men were engaged in business. Almost always, those women who conducted business were in some unusual marital situation in which no male representative was available.

F. By about 1300 B.C., texts inform us of an increasing economic polarization at Nuzi.

1. Agricultural land was subdivided into smaller and smaller plots, and the majority of land was owned by just a few individuals.

2. This doesn't really explain the decline of the city, but shortly afterward, Nuzi was abandoned.

V. City life in the 2nd millennium B.C. in Mesopotamia drew together people of many professions and incomes, and we have a wide range of written and archaeological evidence that informs us about urbanism.

Essential Reading:

Marc Van De Mieroop, *The Ancient Mesopotamian City*, pp. 63–99.

Elizabeth Stone, "The Development of cities in Ancient Mesopotamia," in *CANE*, vol. I, pp. 235–248.

Supplementary Reading:

Elizabeth C. Stone and Paul Zimansky, "Mesopotamian Cities and Countryside," in *A Companion to the Ancient Near East,* pp. 141-154.

Questions to Consider:

1. What features of Mesopotamian culture and life required urbanization to thrive?

2. What conditions might have made it possible—or necessary—for women to own property?

Lecture Seventeen—Transcript
Life in a Mesopotamian City

We saw in the last lecture that the Ur III period was prosperous and culturally vibrant, but that most of our evidence came from the palace—specifically, from the reign of Shulgi. In this lecture, I would like to return to one of our themes of the course—urbanism— to see what developments have occurred since we last explored the topic in the Uruk era about a millennium ago. We know how important public institutions were in cities, the best informed about the temple and also had become increasingly well informed about the palace, which supported, together with the temple, a large workforce that could provide work and food for the poorest members of the city. What can we reconstruct about the rest of the city? Keep in mind that most of our archaeological evidence is richest for temples and palaces, and so what survives, what has even been excavated in the rest of these enormous tells, is very scattered. So, as I talk about cities in the 2nd millennium, I'm going to extrapolate from several centuries and from many different sites to create a picture. Texts fill in some of the gaps that archeological evidence leaves for us, but there are still many questions that remain.

We will begin on a small scale by looking at the house and its occupants and then move to the local government. I have to warn you that this an especially vague aspect of urban life that we would like to be better informed about. Then, I will move on to discuss the different professions that are attested for cities and, finally, end with two studies of specific cities—Sippar and Nuzi. Keep in mind that one of the reasons we chose the aspect of urbanism to explore in this course is to understand that while political events that seemed momentous to us were occurring, most people in Mesopotamia continued living their lives relatively unaffected by what happened among the political elite. So, it's important to keep returning to this theme to keep in mind what the average citizen of Sumer would have been doing while Shulgi was rampaging around building temples.

Cities can be understood as large versions of individual households and so any study of an individual household, both the occupants and the structure itself, is important for our understanding of the city as a whole. Fathers were the undisputed head of the household and they lived surrounded by their family. Parents, sons, their son's wives, and sometimes their children, and any unmarried daughters would live together in one household. So, it's an extended family, but it's not a vast extended family. It's usually just no more than three generations at most. Fathers arranged the marriage of both their sons and their daughters. Women were married in their late teens, men in their late twenties, so there's about a 10-year age gap in the age of first marriage.

The groom's family would give a gift to the family of the bride. In the Early Dynastic era, this consisted of large quantities of food meant to provide for the wedding feast or for the family. Later, by the 18th century, this was silver in an amount equal to the dowry given to the groom by the bride's father. The dowry was a gift given by the father of the bride to support her. It was supposed to ensure that she didn't get married and then her husband lost his job, lost his livelihood, and she and her children would be left to starve. Instead, the dowry was meant to provide the necessities for her. It was overseen by the groom, by the husband, but in the event of divorce, the dowry would have to be returned to the bride's family. We'll come back to this idea when we discuss laws because dowries are often the subjects of legal disputes. It was customary to take only one wife, unless she was unable to have children, in which case, a second wife could be taken by a husband although he could also use another way of resolving the problem—adoption. We know that there are many records of adoptions; often, a family member—say, a nephew or a cousin—or some friend's child would be adopted.

Slaves were an accepted part of Mesopotamian life and they were acquired in many ways, as prisoners of war or infants bought from parents in times of financial crisis, but most of the slaves who are recorded were enslaved because they were paying off a debt. So, someone who needed a loan would offer themselves, their family, as surety for the loan. When they fell behind, they would be enslaved to pay off with the labor necessary to complete the loan. Theoretically, this debt slavery could be temporary, but we know that, in fact, it was very difficult for those who had been enslaved for debt to work their way out without some legal recourse. Families of slaves are known and they were sold and separated; children of a slave woman could be sold at very young ages.

This multi-generational household resulted in very flexible house plans, with rooms added when necessary or affordable. Archaeologists can trace the history of a house by the alterations to the plan. So, when a family expands or acquires more land, the house gets bigger. What we can't know was whether the same family stayed in the house or whether some other family came in, bought the house, and then expanded it to suit their own needs. A typical house plan is arranged around an open courtyard in the center of the house, which would provide light and air. The purpose of the rooms off this courtyard usually can't be identified from the plans of the house, the floor plans or even the remains, because houses were cleared out when they were sold or rebuilt just like today. So, there are very few objects that help us understand what went on in the different rooms.

There are two exceptions to this rule. The first is weaving, which usually occurred in the courtyard of the house, so the weaver would have access to light and air during the process. We find weaving implements in the corners of the courtyard. For example, loom weights—which would be used to hold the wool to keep it taut at the back of the loom while the weaver was creating a textile—are a common find for an archaeologist and so that helps us identify where weaving would take place. The second exception to room identification is that we can usually figure out where the kitchen was because the ground is blackened by the fire. Houses could be either owned or rented, and we have a rental agreement from the 5th century B.C. that notes that the tenant was also a builder. He received a reduced rent in exchange for repairs made to the building. If the tenant did not complete the repairs, he would have to pay the full rate. So, the landlord must have been very excited that he could get this professional to spruce up the place during the year that he was also receiving rent.

The titles of many different local officials are preserved, but it can be quite challenging to understand their specific responsibilities and duties. The mayor was the leader of the court and he often appeared as a witness in lawsuits. The office of mayor is one of those positions that archaeologists wish we knew more about, what a mayor actually did. It seems to be quite different than what mayors do today, but the term is best translated as mayor. The mayor is frequently listed as responsible specifically for prosecuting theft. One text states that a mayor was a middleman, collecting taxes from his people and then sending them on to some other authority—usually, the palace or perhaps a regional governor. This text that records this duty of the mayor was actually from a lawsuit in which the mayor was accused of embezzling those funds and so now the governor of the province was threatening to bring his army to attack the people in order to compel them to pay the taxes that had been embezzled by the mayor.

Another important resource that a mayor would provide would be to deliver the manpower necessary for building projects and other work required by the king, perhaps even serving in the army. The story of a poor man from Nippur reports an interaction between a mayor and one of his less prosperous citizens. The mayor comes off very poorly in this tale, as politicians often do in satirical literature. The poor man gave a fine goat to the mayor, hoping that the mayor would then in return, in thanks for this, invite the entire family of the poor man to dinner. The motivation behind this is that the poor man realized he could not feed enough members of his family with just one goat, that he needed a larger meal. He thought if he curried favor with the mayor and was rewarded by an invitation to dinner, then more of his family could eat. The mayor doesn't behave quite the way the poor man hoped and, instead, rewarded him with a small cup of cheap beer and some gristly meat that was largely bone. The poor man spends quite a bit of time plotting his revenge, which is elaborate and involves numerous disguises. He first disguises himself as a rich man and then later as a physician. Once he reveals his true identity to the mayor and explains why he has publicly humiliated the mayor— that's the point of the whole story—then, supposedly, there is resolution between the wealthy mayor and the poor man.

Mayors should probably be thought of best as the representatives of the city to the palace and vice versa. They would serve as intermediaries between these two groups. We know that in addition to a mayor, there was an assembly and perhaps even more than one in a large city. A large city might be divided into different districts and each one would have an assembly. The assembly had a leader, whose main purpose was to imprison people, so they formed a legal oversight of the city or their district. There's no indication of who could belong to an assembly; it's generally assumed that it was only men who would participate in this legal or political role because no women are mentioned, but that's an argument from silence, so I don't think we should assume that in every case.

Scattered sources reveal that cities were divided into quarters or neighborhoods, and there were probably leaders at this level that oversaw the more mundane needs of a city: keeping streets clear of litter, policing petty crime, issues like that. Again, when we discuss laws, we'll see some of the problems that affected urban life and that these would be resolved through the assemblies or through adjudication at the local level. There are many titles of officials recorded in texts, so we know that there was a thriving urban bureaucracy, but the terms don't help us understand exactly how this bureaucracy works or what the social or political hierarchy of the leaders was.

Let's move now to look at what the rest of the people are doing in the city; if they're not members of the assembly, what are their professions? We've spoken most about agricultural workers, weavers, and priests, but texts record many ways of making a living. Some of these professions were seasonal, so we think immediately of the agricultural workers who had months when their services weren't necessary. They might have some other way of getting income during the downtime for the agricultural season. The food industry required bakers, butchers, gardeners, brewers, and tavern keepers and servers—and these last two were usually women, the tavern keepers and servers. Architects, craftsmen, masons, and carpenters all created homes and other buildings, and wreckers would tear down old structures to make way for new ones. Boat-makers created river craft and sailors helped merchants ply their trade. Foresters and wood collectors would supply the timber for the vessels. Gatekeepers controlled the access to a city, a temple, or a palace. Artisans, such as basket makers, leatherworkers, furniture makers, or seal cutters, would produce the crafts for private citizens or the palace; there would be a different level of luxuriousness based on who the customer was.

Certain quarters of the city devoted to craft production can be identified in the archaeological record. If they were especially disruptive—such as tanning, which was quite a smelly process, to make leather—or if they had special technical requirements—such as large kilns to fire pottery—then they would be placed either outside of the city walls or in specific sections that were far from the majority of the urban population. One profession that we could expect to leave physical evidence is a scribe or a scribal school. We've discussed scribal schools in connection with the Ur III period. At Nippur, a home was discovered that seems to be the site of a very small scribal school, so not a large school that was overseen by the palace, but this is the next step up from home schooling. How do we distinguish between a scribal school and just a regular home of a scribe? There are a couple of hints. First of all, there is a wide range of topics written on the tablets that were found in this particular home. Even more compelling are the numerous examples of misspellings and awkward signs that suggest that they were practice tablets by students who were not yet comfortable with the mastery of cuneiform that they would need to carry on their profession.

Centralized craft production is best known from the Ur III period when the administrative documents are so plentiful. At this time, 13,200 weavers were employed by the palace at Ur; most of these were women who would bring their children to the palace while they worked. We can imagine that these would be among the poorest women, perhaps widows who had no other means of support because they would be paid in rations. The rations would be given to them and also to their children. One reason why so many workers were needed was that weaving was a very time-consuming processing; it took a total of 400 days to create a garment weighing approximately seven pounds. So, if we have thousands of weavers working simultaneously at the palace, the output would be steady and productive, but it would require a significant amount of labor.

Let's move now to look at a couple of examples of 2nd-millennium cities at Sippar and at Nuzi. These are quite different examples of cities and they give an idea of the range of urban centers that were present in Mesopotamia. At Sippar, in central Mesopotamia, the discovery of different groups of tablets can yield valuable information about family histories and professions. Here, there's been a study of what has survived in the houses. One home belonging to a certain Ur-Utu, who was the chief singer of lamentations of the goddess Annunitum, contained over 2,000 tablets. Remember I've spoken along the way about how difficult it is to study tablets when they are not found in context and here we get a sense of, certainly, an important member of the city of Sippar, but in his house, he left behind 2,000 tablets. This is an important archive for what one individual and his family controlled and the areas that he was active in that required receipts and other official documents. Ur-Utu was quite the real-estate magnate. He owned extensive property in the area of Sippar. The receipts that record the transactions between Ur-Utu and the individuals he bought land for usually supplied a history of the plot of land. So, just like modern deeds, they will note past sales, any divisions of the property—so this gives us a sign of when large pieces of property were cut up into smaller pieces—and then, finally, the current transfer of property is recorded.

Ur-Utu's father, from whom he had inherited the house—which we know from one of the texts—kept copies of numerous contracts for agricultural labor. So, in this house, we have not only the records of Ur-Utu, but also the previous generation is keeping a lot of documentation. We see from these excavations how the records were stored and kept. It would be very illuminating to have more of these personal archives because the way that individuals store information really does give us a sense of what they consider is important and what would be essential for later legal transactions or any other disruption that they might need to get involved in. The reason that we found so many tablets at Ur-Utu's house is that he apparently left in a hurry. Some of the tablets were strewn between several rooms and some fell down the staircase, so there's an indication of a very quick departure. There's also an indication that someone was there tossing tablets around, so rifling through them, and we can imagine Ur-Utu perhaps having to leave town in hurry. We don't know why, but trying to extract from this large archive what documents were important and then tossing the rest aside. If we had just received these tablets on the art market or in a museum, our interpretation would be significantly different than if we had the excavation data associated with it. Now, we know that all of these real-estate records were kept by one person and we know that there were a couple of generations of this one family that were very important in the city of Sippar.

The last city that we will examine is Nuzi, which is really much more of a large village, and it is found in the area near Kirkuk in northeastern Iraq. Nuzi lies in the foothills of the Zagros Mountains; they're only about 10 miles away. If you think way back to our early discussions of geography, you can imagine that this is the area that is much hillier. It's also an area where agriculture can be produced by rainfall, so it's much different than what we see in southern Mesopotamia, which is dependent on irrigation for agricultural harvest. Assyria lies to the west of Nuzi and Babylonia to the south.

There's really nothing especially noteworthy about Nuzi's economy. Its agriculture and trade seem to plug along just as one might expect.

What's exciting about Nuzi is that we don't know what most villages of this size were like. This gives us, really, almost unique insight into what a small city was like. The texts date roughly to the second half of the 2nd millennium. At this point, it is the heartland of Assyrian territory, but at this time, Assyria was not the dominant political power. The population of Nuzi is estimated to be about 1,600; if you compare this to Uruk's population of at least 40,000 around 3000 B.C., you see that this really is just a very small city on the border of nowhere. The city has three large public complexes and three large suburban villas beyond the walls of the town. A drainage system of terracotta pipes removed rainwater and waste from the buildings to streets or to larger drains. And, manholes could allow the sewers to be cleared, waste went out to the sides of the city on the tell on which the city was built.

The largest building was the administrative center, which was not a palace, but probably where the assembly met and the mayor conducted business. This public structure was large, about 130 by 85 yards, and it had over 100 rooms and numerous storage chambers. The business section of this large administrative center had a lot of texts that were excavated there, so we get much of our information about the economy of Nuzi from these storage rooms. The courtyards of the public building were highly decorated and they would be places where most of the population of Nuzi could gather if they had to discuss a certain issue. Living space has also been identified in this public building and it includes a small private chapel with painted walls that are much more elaborately decorated than other areas of the building; there are also a number of texts that were found here. These are the ones that are associated with the mayor's activities, so it was probably where the mayor lived. Among the private buildings, there's a wide range of variety in house type and so there's no real typical house plan. We can identify a wealthy area at Nuzi, and that's in the north and northwest of the town. It's very rare to be able to make distinctions like this because most large cities aren't anywhere near completely excavated, but we can see that the houses in the northern quarter are larger, airier, and better decorated.

The texts from Nuzi are especially informative about women's economic status and we see that women owned real estate in their own name. We have examples of women owning both small single lots with a house or perhaps a plot of land and then larger urban complexes, so several houses or a neighborhood in the city. Women sued and were sued in civil cases over land and in criminal cases concerning property; they won and lost these legal suits. It's important that women were able to own property because, according to all of our written sources and all of our understanding of Mesopotamia to this time, we know that land was a key source to real wealth. So, if women own property, then they too have access to wealth and prosperity. We also see the women of Nuzi arranging marriages of their children. Remember I said that often, or usually, it is the father who arranges these marriages, but at Nuzi we see women doing it, as well. All in all, at Nuzi, women had legal equality with men. They were witnesses and they were treated in the same way when they were called as witnesses; the only exception was that women were not allowed to be judges. This was explicitly forbidden in one of the texts. We also see a parity between men and women when it comes to inheritance. Daughters could inherit the same amount of land as sons could.

All of this seems like a little wonderful haven in northeastern Iraq for women, so let's balance the picture a little bit. Even though we have a lot of texts that describe women's economic activity and their legal activities, on the whole, there were far fewer women than men engaged in business even at Nuzi. Those women who were involved in business were almost always in some unusual marital situation where there was no male representative for the family. The most common example is that of a widow whose son was below the age of majority. So there's a young son, small family, and a woman trying to keep the property together for her son to turn over to him.

By about 1300, texts inform us of an increasing economic polarization at Nuzi. There's a noticeable subdivision of agriculture into smaller and smaller plots, owned by a few individuals who buy up the majority of the land. So, the rich are getting richer; the poor are getting poorer. Even though we can trace this development, we don't understand why the city was declining at this time or why it was different than anywhere else. But, shortly after 1300, Nuzi was abandoned.

City life in the 2nd-millennium B.C. Mesopotamia drew together people of many professions and incomes. We see a wide range of written and archaeological evidence that informs us about urbanism.

In the next lecture, we will move to an even more mundane topic: food and drink in Mesopotamia.

Lecture Eighteen
Food and Drink

Scope:

This lecture covers food and drink in Mesopotamia from prehistory to the time of Alexander the Great. The evidence for the food and drink enjoyed by the inhabitants of Mesopotamia comes from artistic representations, archaeological discoveries, scattered written references to feasts sponsored by temples or rulers, and poetry. Ration lists, accounts of royal banquets, and a lexicon of Akkadian and Sumerian terms supply additional evidence. A typical meal probably consisted of staples, such as bread and beer, but the availability of meat and fruit depended on the wealth of the individual or family. We are, as often, most knowledgeable about the diet of kings and the elite; official records note what goods were ordered and describe large feasts sponsored by rulers. Texts also list the rations given to temple or palace workers, giving us insight into the diets of average citizens.

Outline

I.   The rich environment of Mesopotamia supplied a diverse diet for the inhabitants of the region.

    A. Grains, nuts, fruits, and vegetables were fully domesticated by the end of the 3rd millennium B.C. Barley and emmer wheat, barley, and chick peas were all common.

    B. Domesticated animals provided beef, pork, lamb, and goat, but these animals were, for the most part, too valuable to be used regularly for food. Wild animals were probably more common sources of meat.

    C. Rabbits, gazelles, many different birds, and fish were plentiful. Locusts provided another source of protein.

    D. Eggs also supplied protein. One source notes that more than 150,000 eggs and 50,000 birds were collected as tribute by Shulgi over two years.

    E. Dairy products were available, but it is uncertain how they would have been preserved without spoiling unless they were made into cheese.

F. Onions, leeks, and garlic seasoned dishes, but other spices were costly and mostly available only to the wealthy. Cumin, coriander, and perhaps, mustard were also used.

G. Sesame, linseed, and olive oil were available to enliven recipes. Honey, as far as we know, was not cultivated but may have been collected in the wild.

H. Truffles were a delicacy that could please a ruler; at Mari, a workman delivered truffles to the palace.

I. Dates were popular, and date orchards were among the most highly desired agricultural resources; apples, pears, figs, and pomegranates were also common fruits.

II. Two meals a day, in the morning and evening, were customary. Cult statues of the gods were also served two meals a day.

A. Bread and beer were the staples of most meals. More than 300 Mesopotamian terms for bread have been identified, although no recipes survive.

   1. Added flavorings might include fruit or oils (sesame or olive). We also find references to large loafs, specific shapes, and different grains.

   2. Several clay molds with different shapes and designs have been found in the palace kitchens at Mari.

B. Beer, made of barley, was a nutritious element of a Mesopotamian meal.

   1. The barley would be allowed to sprout, then crushed into a mash that was malted and fermented in large vats.

   2. Once fermentation occurred, the malt was dried, which allowed it to be transported and stored easily. Water and other flavors would be added, such as pomegranate and aniseed, and the liquid would again be fermented in large vats.

   3. Some artistic representations show people drinking from a vat using long straws. Individual beakers were also used.

   4. The alcohol content of beer was not especially high; at its strongest, it would approximate the alcohol content in modern beers.

5. The goddess Ninkasi was the patron deity of brewers, and female brewers are listed regularly.

III. Food preparation used an open fire for broiling and roasting and hot coals for warming.

A. Bread was baked in neighborhood ovens or, for unleavened bread, placed on a heated cylindrical burner made of clay. Covered ovens with domed tops produced enough humidity for leavened bread.

B. Pots and kettles of clay or metal were used for boiling, stewing, and making soups, which were very popular.

C. Braziers were used for cooking strips of meat or vegetables in the home.

IV. Palace archives fill in other details about the Mesopotamian diet and indicate specific occasions when rulers hosted large banquets.

A. Wine is described in some texts, especially in royal archives, and trace analysis of jars provides archaeological evidence for wine. Evidence from Uruk suggests that wine was available earlier in Mesopotamia than scholars had originally believed.

1. Some vines could grow in southern Mesopotamia, although few texts inform us about wine production in the region.

2. Most wine was probably imported; a reference to "wine from Carchemish" hints that wine was identified by different areas.

3. Red and white wines of varying qualities and strengths are listed in the surviving texts.

4. Wine was often sent to a king as a gift, and in turn, he would give wine to his favorite officials. Hammurabi received wine from a ruler "of the kind that he himself would drink."

5. Even at the height of its popularity, wine never replaced beer as the favorite beverage of Mesopotamia.

B. Zimri-Lim, an 18th-century B.C. king of Mari, was justly proud of the icehouse he had built in his palace. Ice was probably brought down from nearby mountains, stored, and used to cool drinks.

C. Kings sponsored feasts on a huge scale to earn support among their people and to impress visitors.

    1. The palace kitchen staff was extensive; it would have to serve many people each day and provide food for special occasions.

    2. The palace was a busy center, receiving envoys and merchants and sponsoring many craft industries; the palace kitchen would need a careful overseer of supplies.

    3. A woman named Ama-Dugga was the keeper of the kitchen at Mari; she is known to us from her cylinder seal, which she used to authorize receipts of oil and grain. Her name appears first during the reign of Yasmah-Adad, but she retained her position when this king was deposed and Zimri-Lim took his place.

    4. We also know from Ama-Dugga's cylinder seal that she kept her identification as a servant of the former king rather than changing her allegiance to Zimri-Lim. She was undoubtedly a powerful woman in the royal household.

V. One example of a banquet sponsored by a king allows us to see what a housekeeper such as Ama-Dugga would have overseen.

    A. The 9th-century B.C. Assyrian king Ashurnasirpal II sponsored a feast for 69,574 people when he opened a new palace he had built; he proudly recorded his generosity in a detailed inscription.

    B. The celebration lasted for 10 days; the guest list included locals and 5,000 foreign ambassadors.

    C. The menu for this feast shows the enormous quantity of food that rulers supplied, with 10,000 sheep, 34,000 types of fowl, 10,000 fish, 10,000 jars of beer, and 10,000 containers of wine.

    D. In addition to food, public banquets of this sort would also supply entertainment for the guests, such as dancing, displays of acrobatics, and music.

    E. Guests included foreign envoys, the local elite, court officials, and the ruler's subjects of all professions and income. Such banquets were memorable occasions that united the king with his people.

VI. Public institutions, such as the palace and temple, were connected with food supply in another venue—providing rations in exchange for labor.

A. We have already considered this responsibility of the political and religious elite with respect to the beveled-rim bowl commonly found in 4th-millennium sites that may have held rations for workers.

B. Ration lists survive from many different periods; the rations varied by age and gender but generally fulfilled the calories necessary for a day's work.

    1. Workers who received rations were usually employed in communal projects, such as constructing temples or palaces or assisting with large agricultural harvests.

    2. Rations averaged about 16 gallons of barley a month for a male worker. Children from ages 10 to 15 would receive 10 gallons of barley, while the elderly got about half of that.

    3. Records indicate that a worker would consume half a gallon of beer and half a gallon of barley per day.

    4. In contrast, when an employer had to pay workers for their labor, a male laborer could receive up to 62.5 gallons of barley a month. Presumably, the worker could sell or barter the excess food.

    5. This system seems to reveal that the men, women, and children supplied with food could not command more in exchange for their work; they were probably the lowest members of society.

C. Scholars have identified some periods of famine, inflation, and siege, which kings rarely reveal in their texts.

Essential Reading:

Jean Bottéro, *The Oldest Cuisine in the World: Cooking in Mesopotamia*.

Stephanie Dalley, *Mari and Karana: Two Old Babylonian Cities*, pp. 78–95.

Questions to Consider:

1. How does food help kings display their wealth and control of resources?

2. What role does food play in the economy?

Lecture Eighteen—Transcript
Food and Drink

In the last lecture, we discussed Mesopotamian cities and the evidence for them that exists in the 2nd millennium B.C. I warned you that I was drawing from sites all over Mesopotamia and combining evidence from a lot of different time periods within the 2nd millennium to create that picture of what city life was like. In today's lecture, Mesopotamian food and drink, I'll be doing the same thing, only I will be drawing from an even broader time period— basically, from prehistory down to the end of our course to try and give a sense of what types of food and drink were enjoyed by Mesopotamians. This would have been a consistent diet that they maintained throughout the entire period of history that we're discussing. And so, it makes sense to draw on as much different evidence as possible.

When we discuss food and drink, we use representations of food and drink in art. We also look at archaeological evidence and scattered written references to feasts that might be sponsored by temples, perhaps by rulers. Sometimes, even poetry can give us an idea of what foods were especially exotic or tasty. The written evidence also comes from ration lists and accounts of royal banquets. There's one text that's especially important for providing a sense of the different types of food that were available; this is an ancient dictionary of Akkadian and Sumerian terms for different foods and, on each, there's a row of Akkadian terms and the corresponding row of Sumerian terms. So, when I say something like we have X number of terms for bread or beer, you'll know that it comes from this one particular dictionary.

Many references to rations or even the types of food eaten and distributed survive, but only a few recipes are known, so our knowledge about Mesopotamian meals is somewhat hindered and we have to use our imagination to think about how a cook would combine the different raw ingredients to create a good meal. Certainly, the rich environment of Mesopotamia supplied a diverse diet for the inhabitants of the region. We talked about how grains, nuts, fruits, and vegetables were domesticated in the prehistoric period, and they were fully domesticated by the end of the 3rd millennium B.C. Barley and emmer wheat were the most readily available grains, and barley appears often in the lists of food collected and distributed. It was one of the most common types of grains. Chickpeas were also especially desired and they are a good source of protein. I add them to stews and I'm sure that this was a common use for them in antiquity, as well.

Domesticated animals could provide beef, pork, lamb, and goat, but we know from other sources that the animals were really too valuable to be used for meat on a regular basis and it was probably much more common to hunt wild animals to provide meat for the table. Rabbits, gazelles, and many different types of birds and fish were plentiful from the areas around the rivers and in the marshes, and even artificial ponds would be stocked with fish when necessary to help supply food for the city. Another, perhaps, less widely used source of protein today would be locusts. One letter to a king reports that there had a plague of locusts, which on the one hand, decimated some of the crops, but did in themselves provide food when they were fried for dinner. Eggs, too, could supply protein; over 150,000 eggs and 50,000 birds were collected in a two-and-a-half-year period by Shulgi. Remember that the Ur III kings required a tax of different resources from different regions of the kingdom and so this particular region supplied birds and eggs that the crown would then either use in the palace household or even distribute at a banquet or to other regions.

Dairy products were, of course, available given the prevalence of goats and sheep and cattle, but it is unclear how they would have been preserved without spoiling unless they were made into cheese. In fact, about 20 different terms for cheese are known. Probably the usual and most frequently used type of cheese was some sort of cream cheese that could be flavored with different spices or other additions. Onions, leeks, and garlic seasoned dishes, but other spices were costly and mostly available to the wealthy. A variety of oils— sesame, linseed, and olive oil—were available to add to dishes or to help use in their preparation. As I said, spices don't show up very often in the texts but cumin, coriander, and perhaps even mustard were available; some very scattered references to those spices being imported from the east have appeared in 6th-century texts. As far as we know, honey was not cultivated, but it may well have been collected in the wild. Honey does appear in the texts, but there aren't any references to beekeepers or bee farms.

Truffles were a delicacy that could please a ruler. At Mari, a workman delivered truffles to the palace probably in hopes for some sort of reward, which he received with the gratitude of the king. Dates were a popular fruit and date orchards were among the most highly desired agricultural resources. Other fruits available were apples, pears, and figs, and pomegranates were quite common.

This list of available foods gives you a sense of the resources, but now let's try to combine them into a meal and get a better understanding of how the Mesopotamians ate. Two meals a day—one in the morning and one in the evening—were customary and you might remember that when we discussed temples, I said the gods' cult statues received two meals a day, as well, just like humans. Bread and beer were the staples of most meals. Over 300 different Mesopotamian terms for bread have been identified. No recipes survive, unfortunately, but bakers probably added different ingredients to bread to create this variety of types. We know that some of the flavorings used were fruit; some cut-up dates or pomegranates were even used in bread. Different types of oils—sesame and olive oil are known to be added to bread to create a more savory bread. The terms also refer to the size—a large loaf or a small loaf—and even loaves of bread of specific shapes or perhaps using different grains. All of these would be combined to create enough bread that would please anyone of the most discerning taste. So, you can see that even though bread is one of the staples of Mesopotamian diet, you're not eating the same loaf every single day for your entire life. You have a wide range of choices.

Several clay molds with different shapes and designs were found in the palace kitchens at Mari and some scholars suggest that they were used to make some of these decorative breads that I've just been talking about. So, the shapes of molds there found include fish. There's a set of molds that shows concentric circles. It's possible, other scholars believe, that the molds were serving dishes or maybe even used to make some other sort of food, maybe a cheese or a jelly of some sort. To my mind, it doesn't really matter what the specific use of the mold was; it shows that food was being manipulated to please the eye, as well as the palate.

The other staple of Mesopotamian diet was beer. Beer made of barley would provide a very nutritious element to a Mesopotamian meal. Beer could be made at home or on a larger scale, but we know most about the individual brewers. It was made at home from barley, which would be allowed to sprout, and then the brewer would crush them into a mash that was malted and fermented in a large vat. Once the fermentation occurred, the malt was dried, and this would allow it to be transported or stored very easily; so, you could send the raw ingredients for your beer up the river or you could just keep it over the course of a winter. When you wanted to make beer, you would add water and sometimes other flavors; we know that pomegranate and aniseed—a sort of licorice taste to the beer—are mentioned. Then, once the water was added, once again, the beer would be fermented in a large storage vat and the dregs would settle there. The result is beer, which could be sold in taverns or used at home.

Specific brews are described as especially sweet or old, and we assume that old means good in this case. Some artistic representations show drinkers drinking beer from a large vat. There are several drinkers who sit around the vat, which is placed on the ground, and each drinker has their own long straw, so it really is a communal beverage. We also know that individual beakers were used for beer, so it was not always this communal drinking that we see in some of the earliest representations. The alcohol content of beer was not especially high. At its strongest, it would approximate the alcohol content in modern beers. The goddess Ninkasi was the patron deity of brewers and female brewers are listed regularly. They are also associated with taverns; if you remember we met a female tavern keeper, Siduri, in the Epic of Gilgamesh, and she provided our earliest evidence for the wisdom of a barkeep when she tried to prevent Gilgamesh from going on his fruitless quest for immortality.

Food preparation used fire in many different ways. Food could be broiled or roasted over an open flame or warmed with the judicious use of hot coals. Bread was baked in neighborhood ovens and you remember that bakers were one of the professions that we discussed in the previous lecture. A neighborhood oven would allow a lot of bread to be made without heating up a number of different houses, and this is still a common practice in the Near East today where bread is made and bought on a daily basis rather than made at home. There are examples of home bakeries; bread could be made on a clay cylindrical burner that got very hot, so it would be placed over a fire. The bread was placed at the top, so it would create unleavened bread, flat bread that could be used as we use wraps today. There are also ovens that are covered and have a domed top, so this would provide enough humidity to produce leavened bread. Pots and kettles of clay or metal would be used for boiling, stewing, and soups, which we know were very popular. Braziers for cooking strips of meat and vegetables provided a sort of small, portable kitchen equipment. Again, this would allow the home chef to adapt to the environment. If it was especially hot outside, you don't want to build a large fire over an oven that's inside. You want to have the smallest cooking space necessary and so these little hibachis would have served the purpose quite well.

Palace archives fill in other details about Mesopotamian diet and also indicate specific occasions when rulers hosted large banquets. Wine is described in some of these texts, almost always in a royal archive rather than in a private text. There is archaeological evidence for wine, specifically from the analysis of jars that have been discovered. You might recall that I mentioned that a fairly recent discovery uncovered the remnants of wine in jars at Uruk. That was by far our earliest indication for the use of wine in Mesopotamia, which until this archaeological evidence emerged, wine was thought to appear somewhere over the course of the 2nd millennium and to be a significantly less important beverage than beer. We know that some vines grew in southern Mesopotamia, but there is very little evidence in contrast to the evidence for beer making that informs us about wine production in Mesopotamia itself. Most wine, when it appears in our documents, was imported. We get references to perhaps certain vintages, such as "wine from Carchemish," which is in Anatolia, that may suggest that wine was identified by specific regions, just as it is today.

We have descriptions of red wine, white wine, and wine of different qualities. So, at one of these royal banquets, the best wine is reserved for the king and the rest of the guests get a much lesser quality of wine. Also, there's wine of different strengths; some wine is described as especially strong, while other wine is sweet or very clear. Wine was often sent to a king as a gift, usually from another king. In turn, the recipient of the wine would give it to his favorite officials. Hammurabi received wine from a ruler "of the kind that he himself would drink." So, we see that this is one of those luxury goods that kings liked to exchange to help solidify diplomatic alliances or create a connection between them. Assyrian rulers of the 1st millennium B.C. were especially fond of receiving large gifts of wine from either provincial officials or from other rulers. Even at the height of its popularity, there's no evidence that wine ever replaced beer as the beverage of choice in Mesopotamia.

The 18th-century B.C. king of Mari, Zimri-Lim, was justly proud of his icehouse, which he had built in his palace along the northern Euphrates. An inscription on the foundation stone of the icehouse has been discovered and it credits Zimri-Lim as "the builder of an ice-house, which no previous king had ever built, on the banks of the Euphrates." Letters from the previous king of Mari whom Zimri-Lim supplanted, Yasmah-Adad, had also referred to ice. Yasmah-Adad was quite the gourmand. He often referred to food and wine in his text. He was very concerned with his particular diet and making sure he got the best of everything. So, it's not surprising that he would also be interested in getting ice to cool drinks or to preserve food. Yasmah-Adad's father advised him from the city of Ashur to "give orders to the cup bearer's servants…and make them collect the ice, let them wash it free of twigs and dung and dirt." So, the ice was probably collected from a mountain and then brought down to Mari where it would be stored and wrapped in some way. Yasmah-Adad's father also castigates him about a lot of other details of his rule and we'll come to that in a later lecture, as well. We know that ice was used specifically to cool drinks—both wine and fruit drinks are mentioned as being cooled by ice—and this would have been quite refreshing on a hot summer day along the northern Euphrates.

Kings sponsored feasts on a huge scale and this would earn them support among their own people and also impress visitors. The palace kitchen staff was quite extensive because it would have to serve many people on a daily basis and also, on these special occasions, provide food for tens of thousands of visitors. The palace was always a busy center, receiving envoys, merchants, as well as sponsoring many different craft industries; they would need to have someone who could oversee its kitchen, the supplies received, and how they were distributed. A woman named Ama-Dugga was the keeper of the kitchen at Mari. Her name appears first during the reign of Yasmah-Adad, who was so concerned with his tummy and his ice, and she retained her position even when the king was deposed and Zimri-Lim took over the palace. Her name is known from her cylinder seal, which is used to authorize receipts of oil and grain. This minor piece of evidence informs us that, first of all, the palace officials and staff could stay despite whoever was on the throne at the time. Considering how large a palace would be, it's not surprising that a ruler would want someone with experience. Another detail about Ama-Dugga is that her cylinder seal reveals her identification as the servant of Yasmah-Adad rather than the servant of Zimri-Lim. So, even though there is this change of ruler, Ama-Dugga continues to describe herself by her earlier king. She must have been a very powerful woman to be able to do this in the royal household.

Let's look at one example of a banquet sponsored by a king to give us a sense of what a housekeeper like Ama-Dugga would have overseen. The 9th-century B.C. Assyrian king Ashurnasirpal II sponsored a feast at the opening of his new capital for 69,574 people. He proudly recorded his generosity in an inscription that described the event in detail. The celebration lasted for 10 days; the guest list included both locals—his Assyrian subjects—and 5,000 foreign ambassadors. By this point, the Assyrians were quite a powerful nation and so they could encourage their provinces to send dignitaries for an occasion such as this. The menu for this feast shows the enormous quantity of food that a ruler supplied. Ashurnasirpal II provided 10,000 sheep, 34,000 types of fowl, 10,000 fish, and other types of meat. The guests would sate their thirst with 10,000 jars of beer, the size isn't given, and 10,000 containers of wine. In addition to food, public banquets like this would also supply entertainment. We know of dancing, acrobats, and musicians would be there to entertain the guests. The feast was another occasion for a ruler to demonstrate both his wealth and generosity. At the same time, a feast like this would encourage his people to be especially favorable towards the king. After all, when you leave a dinner and you've had a lot of food and lots to drink, you often have goodwill towards your host. The foreign envoys, the local elite, the court officials, and members of the king's kingdom would have a memorable occasion on which they could meet the king. They would eat with him and that, too, would create a connection between the ruler and his people.

Public institutions, like the palace and the temple, were connected with food supply in another venue, providing rations in exchange for labor. If you think back to the 4th millennium B.C., we've already considered this responsibility of both the ruling and the religious elite. The beveled-rim bowl that we discussed, this disposable container that some scholars believe was a way for grain or beer to be dispersed to workers, was very prevalent in the late 4th millennium B.C. We saw that provided some archaeological evidence for the temple's role in distributing food.

Ration lists survive from many different periods and the rations varied by the age and the gender of the individual, but all of them fulfilled the calories necessary for a day's work. These workers were usually employed in communal projects such as building temples or palaces or large agricultural harvests. They might even clear irrigation canals to bring this abundance to the table. The rations given in return for labor averaged about 16 gallons of barley a month for a male worker. Children, from the age of 10–15, would receive 10 gallons of barley, and the elderly got about half of that. The records indicate that a worker would consume half a gallon of beer and half a gallon of barley per day. In contrast, when an employer had to pay workers for their labor rather than simply providing rations, a male laborer could receive up to 62.5 gallons of barley a month. Presumably, the worker could then sell or barter the excess food and that could supplement his income. We see that those workers who were given rations could not command more in exchange for their work and they were probably the lowest and most vulnerable members of society. So, when we see a division by age, such as by the age of the children—and children as young as five are recorded in these rations list—and the elderly, there are these distinctions in what rations they receive. We also are reminded that the temple and the palace had this duty to provide food for their people. The way that they did this was to put them to work in different tasks.

We've seen how the temple and the king are ordered to supply food for their people, especially those who can't easily supply food for themselves. There are also occasions when, somehow, the king could not supply food for his workers and these don't receive much attention in the text because kings don't like to reveal their weaknesses. But, we can identify certain periods of famine and I think I mentioned one of these at the end of the Ur III Dynasty; the last king, Ibi-Sin, was facing a widespread famine in his kingdom and he sent letters to a general begging the general to send him food so that he could supply the people at Ur with bread. He demanded the food at any price, so we get a sense that there were definitely times when there was inflation for the basic necessities of life.

Another occasion that would cause a disruption of the food supply would be when cities were besieged. This is one of the drawbacks to city life that when, as war increased in the 2nd and 1st millennium, cities would more often be besieged by rulers who were trying to control a large territory. And so, an army encamped around the city would prevent workers from going out to their fields and any food that would supply those who were cooped up behind the city walls, protected by the walls, had to be brought in before the siege began. Eventually, the food will run out, in no small part because there were more people behind the city depending on its protection. And so, as we look at military records, we can usually figure out when the food, sometimes even the water supply, ran out in the city. When Hammurabi was encamped around the city of Larsa, the siege lasted about six months before food ran out and this would be the occasion of surrender of the city.This survey of food allows us to explore both the local and exotic resources that were available for the meals enjoyed in Mesopotamia. Sometimes when we think of the ancient world, we think that everyone was eating a sort of tasteless mush, a very bleak diet of barely cooked meat. In fact, the texts let us imagine meals much closer to the reality of modern Middle Eastern dishes with a lot of variety and a lot of different tastes and textures. We've also learned that food was a commodity exchanged for work or as a treat given by a ruler to his people on the occasion of a banquet. It could also be the weak link in the defense of the city when a city was under siege.

I'd like you to keep in mind the image of the city and daily life that we've been creating over the past couple of lectures now as we move back to a more historical narrative. In the next lecture, we will begin by a focus on a specific aspect of the Assyrian economy; the merchants who helped create and expand a wide and thriving trade network in northern Mesopotamia. Then, we will start to look at the first hints of the Assyrian military strength that appears for the first time at the end of the 2nd millennium.

Lecture Nineteen
Assyrian Trade Networks

Scope:

We now turn to an unusually specific study of merchant activity in the early 2nd millennium conducted by traders from Ashur (sometimes pronounced or written as *Assur*), a central trading post on the Tigris River that connected routes from southern Mesopotamia west to the Mediterranean. Later on, Ashur would become the capital city of the Assyrian Empire. The documents of the Old Assyrian period (so-called in contrast to the Neo-Assyrian era of the 1st millennium B.C.) allow us to study trade as a private enterprise, rather than as part of a statewide bureaucracy. The 20,000 or so tablets that comprise this evidence were found at an outpost of Assyrian trade, Kanesh (modern-day Kültepe), in central Anatolia. In these texts, we see evidence of an international trade network in textiles, tin, silver, and gold. Merchants loaded donkey caravans in Ashur and traveled west to reach Kanesh. Families of merchants often conducted this trade, with a brother, uncle, or son moving to Kanesh, while the rest of family remained in Ashur. Women were actively engaged in producing textiles. Despite the frequent disasters and risky nature of this enterprise, profits apparently were so tempting that they proved to be irresistible to the merchants involved.

Outline

I. In Kanesh, Assyrian merchants functioned independently in a *karum*, that is, a port or colony.

    A. The word *karum* also seems to be used to describe any marketplace or harbor; we can think of it as an independently functioning sector of a city with its own economic, legal, and social organization separate from local government.

    B. The *karum* of Kanesh was the largest of several Assyrian *karums* that reported to the Kanesh administrators; the *karums* were in direct contact with the Assyrian king and, more often, the city assembly of Ashur.

C. The *karum* was a lower city of sorts at Kanesh, physically separate from the mound that marks the area where the Anatolian population lived. This distance did not prevent social interaction between Assyrian merchants and the local population.

D. Local Anatolian rulers at Kanesh lived in palaces in the upper city; these would be the officials to whom the Assyrian merchants paid taxes and gave the rights to the best merchandise.

  1. Although such agreements have not been found, their existence has been derived from the taxes that were imposed: usually a 5 percent charge, 10 percent preferential duty for the palace, and transit fees.

  2. In return, the merchants had freedom of movement and were protected from raids and robbery.

E. The Assyrian merchants had their own judicial and bureaucratic system that was much like the civic assembly in Ashur. Letters refer to a central office in Kanesh, which has not yet been uncovered. If it is found, it may reveal critical evidence for Assyrian political and legal offices.

F. The homes of the Assyrian merchants were generous in size, with four or five rooms situated around a reception room and often with a second story.

G. A massive fire destroyed the city around 1830 B.C.; this disaster preserved the tablets. Kanesh was abandoned for about 50 years before the settlement was reoccupied, also by Assyrian merchants.

II. The texts that survive from Kanesh were concerned with commercial issues, along with some records of trials or other legal problems. The majority of the tablets were dug up illegally before the modern Turkish excavations began, leaving us with no archaeological context for the texts.

A. Those texts that have been excavated *in situ* show that houses had archive rooms, where tablets were stored on shelves or in very large jars.

B. An archive of a merchant named Ashur-Nada contained several hundred texts, including letters from his father, who oversaw trade arrangements for the family; letters from other *karums* or towns; contracts with customers; receipts for taxes and merchandise; and legal documents.

C. Most of the tablets date to the late 19th and early 20th centuries B.C., the high point of Assyrian merchant activity in the city.

III. The trading system described in the Karum Kanesh texts involved the exchange of goods from southern Mesopotamia to Anatolia.

  A. Assyrian merchants focused on a few specific goods, especially tin and textiles.

    1. Tin was an essential metal for bronze-making and was most readily available from Afghanistan and Iran.

    2. Textiles from Babylonia were highly prized as exports. Records note that in a 50-year period, almost 10,000 textiles were imported to Kanesh by Assyrian merchants.

    3. Raw materials for textiles, such as wool and dyes, were also transported, but this business was less profitable than dealing in the finished products.

  B. Goods were transported using caravans of a few hundred donkeys, which brought the tin and textiles to Ashur from different locations, and from there, moved west to Kanesh in Anatolia.

    1. Donkeys could carry approximately 150 pounds of textiles or tin. One text inventories what a donkey carried: 29 textiles of two different varieties and 65 sealed measures of tin, along with loose tin that could be used to pay for emergencies or bribes.

    2. Note that there was no coined money at this time; instead, lump metal—gold, silver, and tin—was used. Non-metal goods, such as textiles, were given a metal value, usually in silver. A *mina*, a little over a pound of metal, is a common weight mentioned in the traders' letters; 60 *shekels* make up a *mina*.

  C. Traders would have hired workers for the trip and paid for their accommodations and equipment. Traders provided donkeys, which could then be sold when the caravan arrived in Kanesh.

1. In addition, taxes or tariffs had to be paid during the trip, but these fees could provide some insurance or protection from theft. If a local ruler was paid taxes, he would reimburse the merchant for losses incurred from theft.
2. Should disaster strike, such as a flood, the merchant alone suffered the losses of goods and equipment.

D. Trips usually took about six weeks between Ashur and Kanesh, and the route was closed during the winter months. Merchandise was sometimes resold to the local palace or to other local agents. Local agents then dispersed the goods to other *karums* to sell.

E. Silver from sales of the goods was sent by donkey back to Ashur.

F. Moneylenders financed the caravans, usually through partnerships of about a dozen people.
1. Half of the total loan would be paid upfront; in one text, this was the equivalent of more than 30 pounds of gold.
2. Interest rates averaged 30 percent, and the period of the loan was 12 years. We can see that moneylenders were guaranteed significant profits.
3. In non-loan records, profits for traders could range from 50–100 percent; thus, the entire business was extremely attractive to those who undertook the risks.

G. The dangers and difficulty of setting up this trade must have been significant. The Assyrian court would likely have negotiated agreements for merchants to travel specific routes.

IV. One of the most interesting aspects of the Kanesh texts are the letters between family members. These suggest that entire families were involved in trade and inform us about effects of long-distance trade on family life.

A. In general, fathers and family elders remained in Ashur to oversee transactions, while the younger males in the family conducted business in Kanesh. The oldest of these men would stay in Kanesh, and other relatives could be divided up among the other *karums* in Anatolia.

B. Wives complained of the long absences of their husbands and the strain on the family, especially their difficulty in providing for their families.

C. Letters from traders to their wives criticized the quality or style of textiles that the wives produced. There were clearly preferences for certain types of textiles.

D. Women emerge as active partners in this trade, as weavers, leaders of the household, and negotiators with other merchants. Letters tell us about women who wrangled with Assyrian tax officials on behalf of their husbands, represented their husbands' interests in legal cases, and paid off their debts.

E. We also learn from letters that traders could disappear, perhaps intentionally on some occasions, when they wanted to default on a loan, or fell victim to crime or accident.

V. Although the political structure of Ashur is poorly attested for the period of the Kanesh merchants, an early hint of Ashur's later prominence occurs about a century later, in the early 18th century, with the rise of Shamshi-Adad (r. c. 1808–1776 B.C.) to the throne of Ashur.

A. As with many successful military rulers, we know little about Shamshi-Adad's origins, although we do know that he came from a northern city, Ekallatum, which has not been discovered. He conquered Ashur and took the throne in 1808 B.C.

B. Ashur was, at this time, probably still an important mercantile center. This focus on trade may have prompted Shamshi-Adad to move west against the rich trading center of Mari.

C. Shamshi-Adad controlled an impressive amount of territory in northern Mesopotamia, about 1,200 miles from the Tigris to Anatolia.

D. He set his two sons, Ishme-Dagan and Yasmah-Adad, on the throne of cities to the east and west, respectively. Yasmah-Adad's activities as ruler of Mari are documented in the archives of that city, and we will discuss them in connection with Hammurabi and the city of Mari.

E. Shamshi-Adad's kingdom did not outlast his reign; when he died in 1776 B.C., the borders of his state were reduced to the region surrounding the city of Ashur. But he and his sons appear regularly in the diplomatic correspondence that survives from this era, a sign of the power of this northern ruler and his state.

F. The reasons for the collapse of the Assyrian state are unknown, but Shamshi-Adad had to face numerous enemies along his borders, and this may have undermined the strength of the state.

G. Assyria will again become an important state in the 13th century and will expand to dominate all of Mesopotamia and the western states along the Levantine coast.

VI. Our first study of the Assyrians draws most heavily on evidence from 500 miles away, in the merchant colony of Kanesh in Anatolia.

A. We saw that families of merchants engaged in a risky but extremely lucrative caravan trade that connected southern Mesopotamia with Anatolia.

B. We have far less evidence for events in Ashur itself, although its interest in trade is marked by Shamshi-Adad's control of Mari.

C. In the next lecture, we will meet one of the figures best known from Mesopotamian history: Hammurabi of Babylon. He will permanently break down the old loyalty to the city-state and lay the foundation for later empires.

Essential Reading:

Marc Van De Mieroop, *A History of the Ancient Near East, ca. 3000–323 BC*, pp. 89–96.

Klaas R. Veenhof, "Kanesh: An Assyrian Colony in Anatolia," in *CANE*, vol. II, pp. 859–872.

Questions to Consider:

1. How does evidence for family-run trade contribute to our understanding of Mesopotamian trade and economy in general?

2. What insights do we gain into the role of women in manufacturing and trade?

Lecture Nineteen—Transcript
Assyrian Trade Networks

For the first two centuries or so of the 2nd millennium B.C., no single ruler or city led Mesopotamia. We've taken advantage of this break in the sources to study aspects of daily life—what life was like in the city and what people were eating and drinking. Now we will turn to an unusually specific study of merchant activity conducted in the early 2nd millennium by traders from Ashur. The city of Ashur is on the Tigris River and at this time is a central trading post that connected routes from southern Mesopotamia west to the Mediterranean. Later on, it will become the capital city of a large empire.

The documents of the Old Assyrian period, so called in contrast to the Neo-Assyrian era of the 1st millennium B.C., are focused solely on private trade rather than political leadership. These sources allow us to study trade as a private enterprise rather than as part of a statewide bureaucracy, which is really how we've been looking at trade up to this point. The old Assyrian records recording this merchant activity are the most detailed and extensive records for any period or any region of the ancient world. The 20,000 or so tablets that comprise this evidence were found at an outpost of Assyrian trade, Kanesh, in central Anatolia. Its modern name is Kültepe and the site has been excavated since the mid-20th century by Turkish archaeologists.

Within this foreign city, the Assyrian merchants functioned independently in a *karum*, which is the Assyrian word for port or colony. Karum also seems to be used to describe any type of marketplace or harbor, so we can think of it as an independently functioning sector of a city with its own economic, legal, and social organization that is kept separate from the local government—sort of like an embassy is today in the modern era. The karum of Kanesh was the largest of several Assyrian karums and the smaller karums would report directly to the Kanesh administrators. They, in turn, would have direct contact with the Assyrian king and, more often, the city assembly of Ashur. So, Kanesh is really the center point of this large trade route.

The karum at Kanesh was a lower city of sorts, physically separate from the mound that marks the area where the local Anatolian population lived. This physical distance did not prevent intermarriage between Assyrian merchants and local women. We shouldn't think of it as a distinct social separation; certainly, the Assyrian would have visited the upper city without any problem. We don't have any records indicating local disputes between ethnic groups. The local Anatolian rulers at Kanesh lived in large palaces in the upper city. They would be the officials to whom the Assyrian merchants paid taxes and gave the rights to the best merchandise, in return for conducting their business in Kanesh. Although the exact treaties reporting this are not discovered, we can derive the information from the taxes that are usually imposed and these are recorded by the Assyrian traders. Usually, there is a 5% charge given to the local rulers and a 10% preferential duty. In other words, the king can have the right to look at the best 10 percent of the goods that he decides he wants to buy. In addition to these taxes, there would be transit dues or fees—and we'll talk about what these were a little bit later on. In return for these taxes and other privileges, the local ruler would protect the merchants against raids, robbery, or any type of hold up, and these were very frequent.

The Assyrian merchants had their own judicial and bureaucratic system that was very much like the civic assembly in Ashur, as it is described in later texts. Remember for this period we don't really have any information for what's happening in Ashur at the time. The letters refer to a central office in Kanesh, and this has not yet been uncovered. If it is found, it may reveal critical evidence for Assyrian political and legal offices. At present, we really only know about private life in the Old Assyrian period and nothing substantial about the government. So, this is a striking contrast with many other periods, such as the Ur III period, where the opposite situation occurs and we know what the king does seemingly at every moment of the day, but we don't know what's happening in the rest of the kingdom. In this case, the lens is turned in the opposite direction. We know what an individual Assyrian family of traders is doing, but we don't know who is king of Assyria at this time.

The homes of the Assyrian merchants are generous in size. There are about four or five rooms on average around a reception room, an open courtyard, and often there is a second story, so there would be a double level for the house. A massive fire and widespread evidence of destruction destroyed the site around 1830 and this preserved the numerous tablets for us, but the site was abandoned for about 50 years before the settlement was reoccupied by Assyrians. They were also merchants, but there were far fewer of them and the trading activity is much more circumscribed than we see in the old Assyrian period. The city of Kanesh, on the other hand, continued to thrive into the Roman era. So, the local settlement continues; it's just the Assyrian karum that is abandoned.

The texts that survive were concerned almost exclusively with commercial issues; some records of trials or other legal problems also are mixed in with the trading records. The majority of these tablets were dug up illegally before the Turkish excavations began and they're scattered in museums throughout the world, so we lack an important archaeological context for these texts. Those that have been excavated in situ show that the houses had special archive rooms, where the tablets were stored on shelves or in very large jars. An archive of a merchant named Ashur-Nada contained several hundred texts with letters from his father, who oversaw the arrangements for their participation in the trade, letters from other karums or towns that engaged in trade or exchange with them, contracts with customers, receipts for taxes and merchandise, and a few other legal documents. Most of the texts date to the late 20th and early 19th century B.C., about 1910–1830, which was the high point of Assyrian merchant activity in the area.

The trading system described in the karum Kanesh texts involved the exchange of goods from southern Mesopotamia to Anatolia. Assyrian merchants focused on a few specific goods, especially tin and textiles. Tin was essential for making bronze and was most readily available from Afghanistan and Iran, so it would come from the east. Textiles from Babylonia were especially highly prized as exports. Records note that in a 50-year period, almost 10,000 textiles were imported to Kanesh by the Assyrian merchants. Sometimes they would also transport the raw materials for textile, such as wool or dyes, but this was a much less profitable commodity than the finished products. The goods were transported using donkey caravans of a few hundred donkeys, which brought the tin and textiles to Ashur from different locations. From Ashur, they would move west to Kanesh in Anatolia. So, think of Ashur as the converging point from which the donkey caravans move north and west to Anatolia. Donkeys could carry approximately 150 pounds of textiles or tin. The letters describe the details of loading the donkey, so we have, again, one of these very illuminating documents that give us specifics that are so exciting. One text describes a donkey carrying 29 textiles of two different varieties—we don't know what they were—65 measures of tin that were sealed, and an amount of loose tin, as well, that could be used to pay for emergencies that might come up or bribes. There was no coined money at this time; instead, lump metal, gold, silver and tin was used. Nonmetal goods, such as textiles, were given a metal value, usually in silver, in order to make a fair exchange. A *mina* is just a little over a pound of metal and this is a very common weight mentioned in the traders' letters; 60 *shekels* would make up a mina.

Traders would have hired workers for the trip, paid for their accommodation and for any equipment necessary. They also had to buy all of these donkeys that were forming the caravan and the donkeys were then sold when they arrived in Kanesh because they would need far fewer to transport the silver that was exchanged for the goods back to Ashur. In addition, there were taxes or tariffs to be paid along the trip. Some of these, as I mentioned, would provide insurance or protection from theft. If a local ruler were paid taxes, these rulers would ensure that merchants were reimbursed for their losses that they would suffer in a theft or robbery of a caravan. Should disaster strike—a flood, for example—the merchant alone suffered the losses of goods and equipment. So, this is going to be a high-risk investment.

Trips usually took about six weeks between Ashur and Kanesh. The route was closed during the winter months because it was too dangerous. The merchandise was sometimes resold to the palace at Kanesh or to other local agents, and then they could disperse the goods to other karums to sell. Silver, from the sale of the goods, was sent back home by donkey, back to Ashur. Moneylenders would finance the caravans usually through partnerships of about a dozen people. Half of the total loan would be paid up front and, in one text, it was the equivalent of over 30 pounds of gold, which was the medium of exchange for loans. So, silver is the most important commodity for individuals, but gold would be used for financing large ventures like this. Interest rates averaged 30% and the period of the loan was 12 years. The moneylender would be guaranteed a profit. In non-loan records, profits that the traders report could range from 50–100%. So, we see that the business was very lucrative and attractive to those who would undertake the risks.

While we see the results of this trade established in the late 20th century, we have to think of the first travelers who began to set up this arrangement. The dangers and the difficulty of establishing the trade route and establishing the connections with local rulers must have been quite significant. We can think of it as early venture trading. The Assyrian court would negotiate agreements for merchants to travel on specific roads; again, we don't have these agreements, especially from the Assyrian side, just the records of the payment to local rulers.

One of the most exciting aspects of the karum Kanesh texts is the letters between family members. Here is where we see that trading and this merchant activity that flourished was really a family business. The entire families would be involved and so we also get some important information about the effects of this long-distance trade, all of this travel on family life, what happened back home, who was in charge, what members of the family were sent to Kanesh, and which were sent even farther to other karums in Anatolia. In general, fathers and family elders remained in Ashur and they would oversee the entire trade transaction. They would be the ones who would decide which younger members of the family—sons, nephews, or cousins—would be sent out to Anatolia. Usually, the oldest of these male members of the family would stay in Kanesh, so we'll say the oldest son is in Kanesh. He is reporting to his father in Ashur and he, the son in Kanesh, is overseeing the relatives at the other karums in Anatolia.

Wives play an important role in this trade, as well. We see their role in the letters. Wives complained of the long absences of their husbands and the strain on their family, especially their difficulty in providing for the family; getting enough money and getting a steady supply of money was a constant problem for the people who stayed back home in Ashur. One Assyrian woman notes that since her husband left, "a terrible famine has hit the city. You did not leave me any barley. I need to keep on buying barley for our food. Where is the extravagance that you keep on writing about? We have nothing to eat...I live in an empty house and the seasons are changing. Be sure that you send me the value of my textiles in silver, so that I can buy at least ten measures of barley." This letter is interesting because it shows, first of all, that the wife felt that the textiles she sent were her property, so she is asking to be paid for what she has contributed to this trade. It also indicates that the husband, apparently in some letter that was missing, had been castigating the wife for spending money too extravagantly, that she was costing him too much money and asking for too much. But, her response is that events have changed in Ashur since he left, and of course this is one of the common problems when families are separated and communication is not easy. There can be some disaster that strikes at one end or the other and the family simply doesn't know about it.

A number of letters from traders to their wives criticize the quality or the style of the textiles that they have sent. We see in these letters that textiles and women are, once again, combined and intertwined as a major profession for women. There were clearly certain types of textiles that were preferred in Anatolia. The most detailed example of this is a letter from a man named Puzur-Ashur to his wife Waqartum. He writes:

> One mina of silver…Ashur-Idi is bringing you under my seal. The fine textile which you sent me, keep producing similar textiles and send them to me with Ashur-Idi and I will send you half a mina a piece…Compared with the previous textile which you sent me, process one mina of wool extra in each piece, but keep them thin!…The Abarnian textile which you sent me—a similar one you should not again send me…If you don't manage to make fine textiles…buy them for me and send them to me. A complete textile which you send should be nine cubits long and eight cubits wide.

This is a very detailed request from a husband; we don't often get this level of concern from the husband. It shows that both the quality of the textiles had to be of a certain level, so when he says that he wants a textile woven with an extra mina of wool, that means that he wants a tighter garment—or a rug, if that's what she's making—that uses more wool. But, he then follows up by saying it should be kept thin. So, he wants her to basically do the impossible—make a higher quality garment, but keep it as thin as possible so the profit margin stays high.

We also see from this letter the value of these textiles and it's hard to gauge what the value of work was in antiquity, so we use these specifics. A half mina for a textile that is nine cubits long and eight cubits wide can help us try and work out what the value of work was considered. It's still a pretty difficult process. We see from these letters that women emerge as very active partners in trade, as weavers, as the leaders of the household in Ashur, and as negotiators with other merchants. So, women really are the representatives of their husbands while they are away. This connects very well with the evidence we got from Nuzi where we saw that widows, for example, could establish negotiations for marriage or be involved in legal cases. If there were no male representative alive for them, then the woman would do it. The same situation occurs in Ashur. We have letters from women who wrangled with Assyrian tax officials on behalf of their husbands, who represented their husbands' interests in legal cases, and even paid off their debts. These Assyrian wives who were married to merchants were obviously very independent women who could govern the household in the absence of their husbands and probably many other male members of their family. We also learn from the letters that traders could disappear, perhaps intentionally on some occasions, if they wanted to default on a loan or saw an attractive Anatolian woman that they preferred to their nagging wife who was constantly asking them for money. They could also fall victim to crime or accident. But, with the difficulty of communication, it's hard for the families to stay in touch.

The evidence from karum Kanesh is important because we see, what we would call today, private enterprise, in contrast to the state-run economy that has been the focus of our investigation of trade so far. Although the political structure of Ashur is poorly attested for this period of the Kanesh merchants, we do get an early hint of Ashur's later prominence about a century after the Kanesh texts in the early 18th century, with the rise of Shamshi-Adad to the throne of Ashur. As with many successful military rulers, we know little about Shamshi-Adad's origins, although we do know that he was not from Ashur, but rather from another city on the Tigris, Ekallatum. This city has not yet been discovered, so we're not exactly sure where it is. Shamshi-Adad appears in the text after he conquers Ashur and takes the throne in 1808 B.C. Ashur was at this time probably still a very important mercantile center. This focus and emphasis on trade may have been the reason that Shamshi-Adad moved west against the city of Mari on the Euphrates River, and he established control of this rich trading center.

Shamshi-Adad would control an impressive amount of territory in northern Mesopotamia during his reign about 1,200 miles from the Tigris to Anatolia. And so, even though this political history is a little confused, we start to see that large powers, large regional states, will become the norm and we'll discuss this in more detail in the next few lectures. Shamshi-Adad set his two sons, Ishme-Dagan and Yasmah-Adad, on the throne of the cities to the east and west, respectively. Yasmah-Adad's activities as the ruler of Mari are documented in the archives of that city; you might remember I mentioned that his father had written him telling him how to collect ice. I also mentioned that Yasmah-Adad was someone who was very concerned with providing a good, rich diet for himself. We will see that he is not a very good ruler, perhaps because of this tendency towards self-indulgence. We'll discuss both of these rulers, Shamshi-Adad and Yasmah-Adad, in connection with Hammurabi and the city of Mari.

Shamshi-Adad's kingdom did not outlast his reign. When he died in 1776 B.C., the borders of his state diminished to the region surrounding the city of Ashur. But, he and his sons will appear regularly in the diplomatic correspondence that survives from this era, and it gives us a sign of the power of the northern ruler and his state. I'd also like you to keep in mind for our future discussions of Assyria that our earliest evidence revolves around its role as a trading center. This may help explain the motivations for creating the large empire of the 1st millennium, which tended to control trade routes. And so, our focus on the old Assyrian merchants, even though it doesn't provide political evidence for the era, does give us a good social background for what the interests of the Assyrians were.

The reasons for the collapse of the Assyrian state are unknown, but Shamshi-Adad had to face numerous enemies along his large borders and this may have eventually undermined the strength of the state. The constant warfare required a lot of demands of labor and this may have had economic repercussions that we don't know about. The written and archaeological records from this area of northern Mesopotamia will be very sparse for the next four centuries. So, we are introduced to Assyria, we get very excited about it because we see all these great merchants and start to see its focus on militarism, and then it just disappears for the next 400 years or so. When Assyria reemerges in the 13th century, it will dominate all of Mesopotamia and the western states along the Levantine coast, so all the way west to Syria Palestine.

Our first study of the Assyrians draws most heavily on evidence that was discovered 500 miles away in Anatolia. The merchant colony of karum Kanesh brings to light the lives of families of merchants who were engaged in a risky but extremely profitable caravan trade that connected southern Mesopotamia and Anatolia. The details of financing, the arduous trips, and the home life in Ashur are preserved in the letters and receipts kept by merchants. Really, it is only through the texts that we have any idea about this level of detail of daily life. Archaeological evidence would never preserve the goods that were involved in this trade, so textiles would not be preserved in the archaeological record, tin would be used. And so, without the texts, we would be missing this great glimpse of really very immediate concerns of family and personal finance. We have a lot less evidence for what's happening in Ashur itself until it is taken over by a foreigner, Shamshi-Adad.

In the next lecture, we will meet one of the figures best known from Mesopotamian history, Hammurabi of Babylon. Hammurabi will come to the throne of the city-state of Babylon. This is a time when, in southern Mesopotamia, the city-states are still the major political unit and the loyalty to the city-state is what keeps the region from unifying. Hammurabi's success as a military leader and his political skill in governing the region break down this old sense of loyalty to the city-state and it breaks it down permanently. So, Hammurabi really lays the foundation for much later empires that are even better known; the Assyrians, the Persians, and even Alexander's Empire all owe their skill and their success in governing to what Hammurabi is able to create in the 18th century.

Lecture Twenty
Hammurabi of Babylon

Scope:

In this lecture, we return to political history again, with the reign of Hammurabi of Babylon (r. 1792–1750 B.C.). When Hammurabi came to the throne as a young man, his territory was hemmed in, to some extent, by stronger men: in the north, Shamshi-Adad of Assyria; Rim-Sin of Larsa in the south; and the Elamites to the east. Hammurabi would create alliances and coalitions to take on these states in order to found a new and impressive kingdom. His long reign gave him time to create a strong personal rule that was largely concerned with justice for his people and, despite his period of successful command, a focus on bringing peace to the era.

Outline

I. Before we begin, we should note that the 18th century B.C. is a very confusing period in Mesopotamian history.

    A. We have looked at the Assyrians and Shamshi-Adad's annexation of Mari and will pick up that thread in the next lecture, which is devoted to Mari's fall to Hammurabi's army.

    B. We now explore the two states that Hammurabi defeated, the Elamites and Rim-Sin of Larsa, victory over which would make him the strongest ruler in southern Mesopotamia since the Akkadian kings Sargon and Naram-Sin.

II. Before Hammurabi, Babylonia was controlled by an Amorite dynasty, but we have little information about the early rulers of this dynasty or the circumstances under which it took control of the throne.

    A. The Amorites were originally a nomadic people from the west of the Euphrates, but they had settled throughout southern Mesopotamia for several generations. We first met them in the Ur III period, when they were described in the sources as a major threat from the western desert.

    B. The Amorites had begun to settle in Babylonian cities in the 300 years since the Ur III kings fell. Their names appear among the city officials, occasionally even as kings. We get no sense that they were seen as foreigners; in fact, sources acknowledge the Amorite heritage of rulers.

C. The Amorites largely adopted the Babylonian culture, but a few elements of their nomadic culture would become influential.

III. At this time, Babylon was just one of many city-states in Babylonia; Hammurabi's father, Sin-Muballit, had integrated smaller cities, such as Kish, under his rule, which made Babylon somewhat larger than other city-states but by no means a major power in the area.

A. Sin-Muballit joined with the leaders of other southern cities to defend against threats from all sides, especially from the powerful Iranian state of Elam. When Hammurabi took the throne on Sin-Muballit's death, he inherited a relatively strong and independent city-state. He would eventually march against several major enemies, but Hammurabi's early reign concentrated on strengthening the economy of Babylon.

B. Hammurabi followed a tradition of issuing a *misharum*, or a royal edict, that forgave certain types of debts.

1. Engaging in trade and agriculture often required loans, and debt was probably widespread.

2. Laws required that interest rates be capped at 20 percent for loans in silver and 33⅓ percent for grain. It was easy to fall behind on these payments, and the penalties were severe.

3. The purpose of the *misharum* was for a king to acknowledge the economic pressures that his subjects faced and to release people from debt slavery.

4. Mercantile loans were explicitly excluded from this generous gesture, and the effects on creditors were probably not severe because the debts that were included in the *misharum* were usually incurred to pay taxes to the king. The edict would affect the royal treasury but would also create goodwill toward the ruler.

5. This "tax cut" represented, for the populace, a brief return to an earlier, more prosperous time. Sometimes a

king would order more than one *misharum* during his reign; Hammurabi did this at least three times during his life.

C. Hammurabi also ensured that the resources for profitable harvests were available; he restored old irrigation canals and dug new ones, including one named after him.

IV. By c. 1765 B.C., Hammurabi felt strong enough to lead attacks against his strongest rivals, first the Elamites, then a few years later, a powerful king in southern Mesopotamia.

A. We are unusually well informed of Hammurabi's planning for these campaigns because numerous letters relating to them have been found.

B. The Elamites had been a strong force in Babylonian and northern Mesopotamian politics even though they did not try to control this territory by military means.

C. By 1765 B.C., Hammurabi challenged the Elamites; he had received aid from other cities, including 2,000 soldiers from Mari, sent by Hammurabi's then-ally Zimri-Lim.

1. Zimri-Lim had some trouble conscripting enough troops to lend to the king of Babylon; his general related to his king that he had to threaten to kill a prisoner if the necessary contingents did not report for service.

2. Zimri-Lim's generosity was probably motivated by gifts or pay given to the troops by Hammurabi, as noted in an official receipt. Some portion of this undoubtedly went to the king.

D. After a year of fighting, the king of Elam surrendered to Hammurabi.

V. The city-state of Larsa commanded much of southern Babylonia; its king, Rim-Sin (1822–1763 B.C.), had challenged and annexed Uruk and other cites. By the time Hammurabi took the throne of Babylon in 1792, Rim-Sin controlled lands from the Persian Gulf north to Nippur.

A. After defeating the Elamites, Hammurabi moved against Rim-Sin, claiming that he was taking the offensive at the request of the gods.

B. Hammurabi captured smaller cities and besieged Larsa with

Rim-Sin inside the city. The siege required an enormous number of troops; according to an account of the battle sent to Zimri-Lim, Rim-Sin marshaled 40,000 troops on his side. Hammurabi's army had to stay for six months before the city ran out of food and Larsa was captured.

C. In Larsa and its territory, Hammurabi established himself in Rim-Sin's palace, began controlling crime and building temples, and issued a *misharum* for the debtors of Larsa.

D. By the later years of his rule, Hammurabi had created a unified regional state in Babylonia; he would extend his reach up the Euphrates River, taking the city of Mari by 1761 B.C.

VI. It is possible to uncover some aspects of Hammurabi's personality.

A. We have the impression that we have complete documentation for Hammurabi's rule, but this is probably misleading. We must remember that we are reading official documents, not a diary, and even Hammurabi's letters were not dictated but written by scribes and approved by the king.

B. That said, several letters and reports about Hammurabi communicate his behavior, especially his bad moods.

1. Envoys were often the target of Hammurabi's outbursts; usually, they had passed on bad news or requests that irritated the king.

2. Hammurabi had little patience for his own officials either. In one letter, he demands that accountants coming from Larsa to Babylon (a distance of about 100 miles) should arrive in two days.

C. Hammurabi engaged in backroom diplomacy and double-dealing, pitting rulers against each other and making promises that he had no intention of keeping.

VII. We turn now to Hammurabi's governance of his kingdom: How did he control and ensure loyalty from such a large territory?

A. Hammurabi made Babylon the political center of his lands, with all taxes sent there.

1. Local leaders would report to officials who were chosen by Hammurabi, and they corresponded regularly with the king.

2. These letters note the productivity of the king's lands, the results of tax collection, and the available supply of labor for Hammurabi's building projects.

B. We have already glimpsed Hammurabi's royal ideology—his use of the *misharum* and the construction of temples—and indeed, these established functions of the king were the hallmark of his rule. Hammurabi also drew on the idea that he was a good shepherd of his people.

C. The king maintained close links with all the gods and did not advance the cult of one specific deity over others.

D. One way that a king served his people was to ensure that they were treated fairly. Hammurabi's law code, the longest surviving law code from Mesopotamia, supplies the best evidence for this aspect of Hammurabi's rule. We will return to this law code in a later lecture.

E. Letters also note Hammurabi's interest in justice, indicating that he interceded on behalf of his subjects even in minor matters.

F. Hammurabi's subjects believed that he was genuinely concerned for their well-being, and he was made a god. This deification probably began in the south, where the concept had become more common.

G. Hammurabi's concern for justice and peace for his people was remembered for centuries after his death. Praise poems note that he "gives the disobedient the death sentence," and he is "the great net that covers evil intent."

H. Hammurabi's reign was clearly successful, and his law code monument has ensured his fame over the generations. The dynasty that he established prospered for another century and a half, although other states in the Near East were becoming more powerful. In 1595 B.C., the city of Babylon was attacked and destroyed by invaders from Anatolia.

VIII. Hammurabi created the largest state since the Akkadian king Naram-Sin in the 23rd century B.C. His long rule helped to unify the region politically in a way that the Akkadians had not been able to achieve.

A. With Hammurabi, the old loyalty to the city-state was finally broken and would not return. Now, a new form of political unit, the territorial or regional state, was established. This shift is a significant break in our history of Mesopotamia and will lay the foundation for the enormous empires of the 1st millennium B.C.

B. Recall, too, that Marduk, the patron deity of Babylon, would replace Enlil as the king of the gods. Even though Hammurabi did not promote the cult of Marduk specifically, it would start to spread and dominate Babylonia. The religious and cultural primacy of Babylonia would continue long after its political dominance had come to an end.

Essential Reading:

Marc Van De Mieroop, *King Hammurabi of Babylon.*

Martha T. Roth, *Law Collections from Mesopotamia and Asia Minor*, pp. 71–142.

Supplementary Reading:

Jean Bottéro, *Mesopotamia: Writing, Reasoning, and the Gods*, pp. 156–184.

Questions to Consider:

1. What can we learn about diplomacy and alliances in Hammurabi's time?

2. What historical events do you think allowed Hammurabi to gain control so quickly?

Lecture Twenty—Transcript
Hammurabi of Babylon

We've had a brief hiatus in the past few lectures as we explored some aspects of daily life—what life was like in the city, what people ate and drank most frequently, and also a very detailed look at the merchant activity of the old Assyrian traders who lived in the karum Kanesh. Now, we will take up our study of political history again and we enter one of the really exciting, but also very complicated periods of Mesopotamian history. In this lecture, we will focus on Hammurabi of Babylon.

Hammurabi came to the throne at a young age. We don't know exactly how old, but he ruled for a long time, so we assume he was relatively young when he took the throne. In the early part of his reign, he was hemmed in, to some extent, by stronger men: in the north, Shamshi-Adad of Assyria—whom we met in the last lecture—Rim-Sin of Larsa in the south—we'll learn more about him shortly—and the Elamites who lived in southwest Iran to the east. Hammurabi will have to create alliances and coalitions to take on these states in order to found a new and impressive territorial state in Mesopotamia. Hammurabi's long reign gave him time to create a strong, personal rule, which was largely concerned with justice for his people. Despite his period of successful military command, he had a focus on bringing peace to the era.

I have to warn you that this is a very confusing period of history. We are going to move back and forth in time, across different regions, because that's what Hammurabi did. You've already met the Assyrians and we discussed briefly Shamshi-Adad's annexation of Mari; we will pick up that thread of history in the next lecture, which is devoted to Mari's fall to Hammurabi's army. In this lecture, I will focus on two important states that Hammurabi defeated: the Elamites and Rim-Sin of Larsa that made him the strongest ruler in southern Mesopotamian since the Akkadian kings, Sargon and Naram-Sin.

Babylonia was controlled at this time by an Amorite dynasty, but we have very little information about the early rulers of this dynasty or the circumstances under which they took control of the throne. The Amorites were originally a nomadic people from the west of the Euphrates, and they had settled over the past three centuries or so in southern Mesopotamia and become very well integrated with urban life. We first met the Amorites in the Ur III period when they were described by the sources as a major threat from the western desert. The Amorite names over the next few centuries become more and more common in our written sources, appearing as city officials and occasionally even a king. Unlike some of the other foreign tribes that we've discussed, who usually brought the end of a kingdom or a dynasty, there is no sense in the sources that the Amorites were foreigners, that they were considered uncivilized at that time. In fact, the sources readily acknowledge the Amorite heritage of the rulers. So, we shouldn't imagine any ethnic tension in Mesopotamian history. The Amorites had largely adopted the Babylonian culture, but a few elements of their own native, nomadic style would become influential.

Babylon at this time was just one of many city-states in Babylonia. Hammurabi's father, Sin-Muballit, had integrated a few smaller cities—such as Kish, which you're familiar with—nearby Babylon under his rule. And so, his city-state was somewhat larger than others, but he was by no means a major power or threat in the area. Sin-Muballit did join with the leaders of other southern cities to defend against threats from all sides, especially from the powerful Iranian state of Elam. When his son, Hammurabi, took the throne on Sin-Muballit's death, he inherited a relatively strong and independent city-state. He would eventually march against many powerful enemies, but the early part of Hammurabi's reign concentrated on strengthening the economy of Babylon.

Hammurabi followed a tradition of issuing a *misharum*, or a royal edict that forgave debts—at least, certain types of debts that were enforced when he came to the throne. We got a glimpse of the money lending profession in the last lecture about the Assyrian traders, and so from that you can easily imagine that debt would be very widespread in the area. Both trade and agriculture required loans in order to conduct business, borrow against the next harvest in order to get seed for the current one. Laws required that interest rates be capped at 20 percent for loans in silver and 33 1/3 percent for grain. It was very easy to fall behind on these payments—say, during a disastrous harvest or a trade caravan that went astray—and the penalties for this were quite severe. The creditors could take the property of the debtors; they could sell them or their children into slavery and force them to work off the debt. So, debt was a major concern for any king taking the throne.

The purpose of the misharum was for a king to acknowledge the economic pressures that his subjects faced. It could release people specifically from debt slavery and the reason for this, according to the edict of a misharum, is that "the king has instituted justice in the land, his freedom is in effect." Mercantile loans were explicitly excluded from this generous gesture by the king and the effects on creditors were probably not as severe as you might expect because the debts that were covered were usually those that had been incurred to pay taxes to the king. So, really, the king is inflicting a penalty on himself and his royal treasury, but the main benefit is the goodwill that is created between the subjects and the ruler. This tax cut of sorts would represent for the populace a brief return to an earlier, more prosperous time in their lives. Sometimes, a king could order a misharum more than once during his reign. In fact, Hammurabi did issue two other misharums during his lifetime. Hammurabi also ensured that the resources for profitable harvests were available. He restored old and dug new irrigation canals, and he even named one after himself so that everyone would know that this particular canal had been brought to them by their new young king, Hammurabi.

By 1765 B.C., Hammurabi felt strong enough to lead attacks against his strongest rivals—first, the Elamites and then, a few years later, a powerful king in southern Mesopotamia. We are unusually well informed of Hammurabi's planning for these attacks because numerous letters with other rulers have been found. We can see how Hammurabi tried to create an alliance and also how he was supplied with troops. The Elamites had been a strong force in Babylonia and even in northern Mesopotamian politics, and this was true despite the fact that they didn't try to physically control the country by military means. Instead, the king of Elam would settle disputes between the rulers of city-states in Babylonia. He would also arrange alliances between them, basically order them to be friends, and he would also demand that the city-states send him troops for his own ambitious expeditions.

Hammurabi was one of the kings who had been ordered early in his reign to send troops to the king of Elam. From these demands, we get a sense of a very powerful ruler off to the east who is able to control what is happening in internal Babylonian politics. In 1765,

Hammurabi had received aid from other cities, including 2,000 troops from Mari, which were sent by Hammurabi's then-ally, the king of Mari, Zimri-Lim. This gave him the strength to lead an attack against the Elamites. Zimri-Lim had some trouble conscripting enough troops to lend to the king of Babylon. His general related to the king that he had to threaten to kill a prisoner if the necessary contingents did not report for service. The threat worked remarkably well, for the general later noted in his report how happy the soldiers were to go to battle for this foreign king, Hammurabi. Zimri-Lim's generosity was probably motivated by the gifts or pay given to the troops by Hammurabi. This is reported in a receipt from Hammurabi's archives. Undoubtedly, some large portion of this gift given by Hammurabi to the soldiers was then conveyed to Zimri-Lim himself. We don't often get details like this about how men were collected to supply an army, so this is a very relevant and important piece of evidence because we see that kings could negotiate with other rulers to help flesh out their own troops.

After a year of fighting, the king of Elam surrendered to Hammurabi. Hammurabi wrote to Zimri-Lim: "The ruler of Elam…wanted to devour the land of Babylon. Now, however, when a king mentions Hammurabi, he says sweetly, 'There is peace'." And so, we see that Hammurabi really did inflict what must have been a very surprising victory against a foreign enemy that no one could have expected him to defeat. This emboldened Hammurabi to take on Rim-Sin, the king of Larsa, who ruled from 1822–1763 B.C.

Rim-Sin was the most successful Mesopotamian ruler in several generations. The city-state of Larsa commanded much of southern Babylonia, as Rim-Sin challenged and annexed the cities of Uruk, Eridu, and other cities that we've become familiar with over time. The year that Hammurabi took the throne of Babylon in 1792 was the year when Rim-Sin controlled lands from the Persian Gulf north to Nippur. So, Rim-Sin reached the height of his power just as Hammurabi took the throne. After the defeat of the Elamites, Hammurabi moved against Rim-Sin, claiming that he was taking the offensive at the request of the gods. Hammurabi quickly moved through the lands of Larsa, capturing smaller cities with apparent ease, and then besieged Larsa, with Rim-Sin and his people inside the city. The siege required an enormous number of troops; we only have Rim-Sin's army accounts and he had marshaled 40,000 troops at his side. We don't know what the size of Hammurabi's army was. We do know that Hammurabi's army had to stay for six months besieging Larsa before the city ran out of food and Larsa was captured, as was Rim-Sin shortly after the city fell.

In Larsa and its old territory, Hammurabi quickly established himself as the new legitimate leader. He occupied Rim-Sin's palace and he began to try and control crime. During the period when Hammurabi and Rim-Sin were fighting—this had been a time of chaos—there were numerous reports of robbers on the highways. Hammurabi, with his army, was able to rid the highways of this danger. Hammurabi also began building temples and he issued a misharum specifically for the debtors of Larsa. This was not an edict that applied to his entire kingdom, but to the area that was most recently acquired and, again, presumably this would bring him the loyalty or at least gratitude of his new subjects. Hammurabi had created a unified regional state in Babylonia. He would extend his reach up the Euphrates River over the next few years, capturing and destroying the city of Mari by 1761 B.C. This is what we'll discuss in the next lecture.

Because of the numerous sources we have from Hammurabi's period, it conveys a sense of his personality. We get an impression of a very complete documentation for Hammurabi's rule. This is probably misleading; just because we have lots of texts for Hammurabi's rule doesn't mean that we know everything about what happened. We also have to keep in mind that these letters and other edicts are official documents; they are not a diary recording Hammurabi's ambition or his personality. Even the letters were not really specifically dictated in that they record Hammurabi's exact words, but they were written by scribes and then approved by the king. It's very much like a speechwriter for a politician who has to give a sense of the personality and the goals of the leader, but these are not the exact words that a president or prime minister might choose. There's also a lot of official speak in these documents, so there are phrases that are repeated frequently and this also weakens the immediacy that we can sometimes think we see in Hammurabi's letters.

That said, there are several letters and reports about Hammurabi that communicate his behavior—usually his moods, which are quite often very bad. He was a short-tempered leader. Those who usually suffered his wrath were envoys from other kings—sometimes his own officials—but, usually, foreign envoys were the targets of Hammurabi's outbursts. One of the reasons that they incurred his wrath is that they might be passing on bad news or requests that irritated the king. Zimri-Lim wanted his troops back after Hammurabi had had them for two years after he conquered the Elamites and Larsa, and Hammurabi didn't want to give them up. Two thousand well-trained soldiers are quite a good weapon to have at your side. On one occasion when Zimri-Lim's emissaries were asking Hammurabi yet again to release his troops, they were not given robes, which were the equivalent of a diplomatic present that would be given from one king to the dignitaries, the representatives of another king. At the same time, even though Zimri-Lim's officials were ignored, officials from another king were given the robes. So, when Zimri-Lim's people complained about their treatment, Hammurabi snapped that, "from the break of dawn, you don't stop annoying me. Are you in charge to decide about garments in my palace? I dress whomever I like and don't dress whomever I dislike. I will never again dress simple messengers at the occasion of a meal." It's hardly something that's going to smooth over a diplomatic relationship.

His own officials also suffered from Hammurabi's impatience, as in this letter describing a demand from Hammurabi that accountants come from Larsa to Babylon—that's a distance of about 100 miles—as soon as possible. Hammurabi writes: "They should travel day and night so that they arrive in Babylon in two days." That would be somewhat arduous for anyone and he sent a follow-up letter demanding to know where they were and why they were sleeping. Like most kings of the era, Hammurabi engaged in backroom diplomacy and double-dealing, pitting rulers against each other and making promises he had no intention of keeping. We'll see this aspect of his personality illustrated most specifically with Zimri-Lim in the next lecture.

Let's turn now to Hammurabi's governance of his kingdom. How could he ensure loyalty and exert control over such a large territory? Remember that no ruler had really been able to do this for very long before, so Hammurabi has a significant task ahead of him. Hammurabi made Babylon the political center of his lands; any taxes that he required would be sent there. Local leaders would report to officials who had been chosen directly by Hammurabi, and they corresponded with the king himself. So, he was a good manager in that he had a very good system of communications with his officials. These letters note the productivity of the king's lands—he now controlled enormous estates in Babylonia—and also the tax collection and the supply of labor that the king needed. Hammurabi specifically engaged in a number of very large building projects, building and maintaining irrigation canals, and also restoring and building new temples. He required an almost constant supply of corvée labor. His officials were supposed to supply this manpower from throughout his kingdom.

We've already gotten a glimpse of Hammurabi's royal ideology with his use of the misharum and the construction of temples; indeed, these established functions of the king were the hallmark of Hammurabi's rule. Hammurabi drew specifically on the idea that he was a good shepherd of his people. He notes on an inscription that, "The dispersed people of the land of Sumer and Akkad, I gathered together and I provided pastures and watering places for them…I made them live in peaceful dwellings." From this inscription—and there are many others that use this phrase of being a good shepherd—we see that Hammurabi takes a very protected sense of his subjects and that he wants to make sure that they live happy, peaceful, and productive lives. Hammurabi also maintained close links with the gods—all of the gods, not just a specific deity that he tried to advance over other cults. When we get to his laws, his very famous law code, we'll see that he lists numerous gods in the prologue.

One way that a king could ensure his people were treated fairly is to oversee their justice. Hammurabi's law code, which is the longest surviving law code from Mesopotamia, supplies the best evidence for this aspect of Hammurabi's rule. The law code dates to the later years of Hammurabi's reign and we can tell this by the list of cities that he claims owe allegiance to him. In the law code, Hammurabi writes that kings should "guide his people correctly, judge their cases and give decisions. May he remove the evil and the wicked from the land, may he make his people happy." We'll see how Hammurabi does this through his laws in a lecture shortly.

Other letters note Hammurabi's interest in justice. He intercedes on behalf of his subjects in relatively minor matters. These letters indicate for us that a king really did provide access to his subjects. If they felt that they had been wronged, whether it be a matter of a loan or some other injustice, they could write to the king and the king would respond. Hammurabi learned of a young man who had been enslaved when a father wrote him. He wrote:

> My son disappeared eight years ago and I did not know if he was alive. I made funerary offerings for him as if he were dead. Now I was told that he is living…in the house of…a goldsmith. I went…but they hid him from me and kept moving him.
>
> [Hammurabi responds:] Now I am sending you a soldier and an official…let them go and bring back your son and the man who kept him in his house for eight years. Have them brought to Babylon.

There, Hammurabi would see them and he would adjudicate the matter. He would make sure that if the son had been enslaved illegally, that he would be restored and probably, according to his law code, that there would be some punishment and penalty given to the father for the loss of his son.

Hammurabi's subjects believed that he was genuinely concerned for their well-being. They made him a god. When we've seen rulers become divine before, usually it comes from themselves; they decide that they are gods. But, Hammurabi's people, probably subjects who lived in the southern Mesopotamian cities that had become more used to the idea that a ruler would be divine, initiated this concept. Children were named after Hammurabi; one young man was named Hammurabi-Ili, which means "Hammurabi is my god." There are several other names of children that include Hammurabi's name in them. This will happen occasionally with other rulers, but Hammurabi is unique in the number of examples of what seem to be genuine honors given to him by his people. His long reign, almost 50 years, would help strengthen this loyalty to him and also the bureaucracy that he had created. You can imagine that when Hammurabi died, some people had never known any other king, so it would be an enormous loss.

This longevity, in connection with Hammurabi's concern for justice and peace for his people, was remembered for centuries after his death and some later sources draw on these themes to describe him.

We've seen praise poems for rulers before—specifically, Shulgi—but the praise poems for Hammurabi really do focus on his concern for justice. One writes that he "gives the disobedient the death sentence" and he is "the great net that covers evil intent." Remember that gods would go on to the battlefield with a battle net to capture their enemies and now the idea has moved to the concept that the king carries a battle net against injustice. The peace and prosperity of Hammurabi's rule are also emphasized in these later sources; it's somewhat ironic that they came at the cost of rather extensive warfare. Some later rulers would even use Hammurabi as a model for their own rule, so they would describe themselves as, like Hammurabi, I, too, am interested in justice. Like Hammurabi, I, too, will bring peace to the region.

Hammurabi's reign was clearly successful and his law code monument has ensured his fame over the generations. The dynasty he established would continue for another century and a half or so, but it did prosper as it had during Hammurabi's rule. There are not as many sources for his successors, and other states in the Near East were becoming much more powerful. So, in 1595 B.C., the city of Babylon was attacked and destroyed by invaders from Anatolia ending the Amorite Dynasty that Hammurabi had brought to such great power.

Hammurabi created the largest state since the Akkadian king Naram-Sin in the 23rd century B.C. His long rule helped to unify the region politically in a way that the Akkadians had never been able to achieve, and the old loyalty to the city-states was finally broken down and this would never return. Now, a new form of political unit, the territorial or regional state, was established. The king would live in a capital city and that would be the main focal point of the state. This shift that occurs during Hammurabi's reign is a significant break in our history of Mesopotamia and it's going to lay the foundation for the large empires of the 1st millennium B.C.

You may also recall in an earlier lecture that I discussed the prominence of Marduk, the patron deity of Babylon, who would replace Enlil as the king of the gods. Even though Hammurabi did not promote the cult of Marduk specifically, it would start to spread in the reign of his successors and eventually dominate Babylonia, becoming its most important cult. All kings of successor states would need to take part in the Babylonian New Year's festival. This indicates for us that the religious and cultural primacy of Babylonia would continue long after its political dominance fell.

In the next lecture, we will continue to study the events of Hammurabi's reign, in this case from the perspective of his ally and later enemy, Zimri-Lim, the king of Mari.

Lecture Twenty-One
Zimri-Lim of Mari

Scope:

In the previous lecture, we discussed the reign of Hammurabi. When he took the throne, the city-state of Babylon was not particularly powerful, and Hammurabi focused his attention on reinforcing the infrastructure of the state. As he grew stronger, he led his army against the powerful states of Elam and Larsa. His success created a large regional state that Hammurabi governed with the same attention to detail that he had given to Babylon. We did not discuss the last major campaign of Hammurabi against the rich state of Mari, in part because there are so many sources for this era that they merit a more detailed study. Another reason is that during this attack, Mari was destroyed, ending the long history of this trading post. In this lecture, we will discuss the turbulent last few decades of Mari's history, in which it was controlled, first, by the Assyrians, then, by the last of its rulers, Zimri-Lim.

Outline

I. The city of Mari was located on the northern Euphrates River, in a position that controlled key trade routes between east and west. Mari was an important power in the Early Dynastic period (c. 2900–2350 B.C.), but it is the city that dates to the 18th century that is best preserved.

   A. One reason for Mari's prosperity was that the city collected taxes on all goods that traveled between Syria and Mesopotamia along the Euphrates River.

   B. In addition, Mari was placed at a key point on the land route that crossed the desert from northern Mesopotamia to southern Syria. Both diplomatic and military contacts between Mari and Mesopotamia are recorded from the Early Dynastic period until Hammurabi destroyed the city.

   C. The Akkadian kings Sargon and Naram-Sin had both considered Mari an important target in their military campaigns and referred to their attempts to control the city.

   D. An Amorite dynasty had taken control of Mari, just as the

Amorites had in Babylonia, in the mid-19th century B.C. Mari was quite prosperous in this period, as we can determine from large building projects, such as the palace and irrigation canals that expanded the fertile land available to support the city.

E. In 1795 B.C., Mari was captured by Shamshi-Adad (r. c. 1808–1776 B.C.), an effective military leader who took the throne of Ashur and dominated the region along the northern Tigris River.

    1. Shamshi-Adad installed his younger son, Yasmah-Adad on the throne in Mari, but he proved to be a disappointing choice. Letters from Shamshi-Adad to his son reprimanded him for failing to organize his household and compared him unfavorably to his older brother.

    2. Even without these letters revealing the strained family dynamics of the Assyrian palace, Yasmah-Adad did not appear to have been an especially successful ruler, and he disappeared almost immediately after his father's death.

II. Zimri-Lim became the new king of Mari in 1776 B.C. He claimed, probably falsely, that he had a blood relationship to the previous Amorite dynasty.

A. Zimri-Lim was a far better administrator than the Assyrian ruler Yasmah-Adad, and the state flourished economically during his reign.

B. Politically, Zimri-Lim reestablished a diplomatic relationship with Babylon and created a network of smaller vassal states that helped Mari thrive. These diplomatic alliances were secured by marriages with Zimri-Lim's daughters.

C. One reason for the focus on diplomacy, rather than military expansion, was that the king of Elam was still very powerful. The Elamite king frequently arranged matters among the lesser kings of Mesopotamia, and Zimri-Lim was one of the rulers who fell under the control of Elam.

III. One of the most contentious issues between Zimri-Lim and Hammurabi was control over the city of Hit on the Euphrates.

A. Hammurabi wanted Hit because it was a source of bitumen, a binding caulk used in boat-building. Hammurabi depended on shipping to transport troops and sustain trade.

B. Zimri-Lim's interest in Hit was that it was the site of a judicial ritual called the "river ordeal."

    1. Accused criminals were taken to Hit, where they or their representatives would have to survive a swimming challenge, such as swimming a long distance underwater or swimming with a millstone around the neck.

    2. If the person completed the assigned task and survived, he or she was deemed innocent; if not, he or she was guilty.

C. After Hammurabi defeated the Elamites, the matter of Hit once again became the subject of debate. A letter to Zimri-Lim from his messenger reported one of Hammurabi's outbursts concerning the control of Hit and his suggestion that the two kings try to share power there.

D. Zimri-Lim had lent 2,000 troops to Hammurabi to help the Babylonians defeat the Elamites; the slow return of this aid also created friction, as did Hammurabi's lukewarm response when Zimri-Lim requested aid in his own border conflicts.

E. As the situation deteriorated, Zimri-Lim grew increasingly nervous, consulting with his wife for help in interpreting oracles to predict what Hammurabi would do. While the oracles reported that Zimri-Lim would be victorious, in the end, he could not overcome the Babylonian army.

F. In 1761 B.C., Hammurabi turned against Zimri-Lim and attacked Mari; the city was destroyed two years later.

IV. The destruction of Mari preserved the six-acre palace, which has been excavated by French archaeologists since the 1930s.

A. The architecture of the complex is well preserved, but the palace was largely emptied of its rich contents by Hammurabi's army before it was destroyed.

B. Walls about 5 to 9 yards thick surrounded the palace, with the main entrance through the north gate. The gate drew visitors into a large courtyard; texts from Mari refer to a "court of palms" in the palace, which may have been this space.

C. The palace complex had 260 rooms. Archaeologists encounter the same problems with identifying the functions of the palace rooms that they have for less grandiose houses, but we can try to speculate based on the level of public versus private access, as well as the wall decorations.

D. An example of these decorations is found on the wall of a smaller courtyard within the palace. This painting has been called the "Investiture of Zimri-Lim" and shows a male standing before the goddess Ishtar as she hands him a scepter.

E. Sanctuaries and chapels to the gods were incorporated into the palace, and several statues of worshippers and deities were left behind when the palace was abandoned.

    1. A limestone statue of a goddess, a little smaller than life-size, shows her holding a water jar in her hands; it is tilted toward the viewer and had a hollow channel to allow water to flow through the jar to create a fountain.

    2. This statue was found in an antechamber to the supposed throne room and may have served as a small shrine.

V. Archives holding about 20,000 records were preserved in the final destruction of Mari.

A. Babylonian officials who occupied the palace after it was first attacked went through the archives, removing most of the letters from Hammurabi to Zimri-Lim.

B. The rest of the palace archives were divided up and labeled; the labels are clay sealings, noting the year of Hammurabi's rule.

C. Letters from Zimri-Lim's wife and queen, Shibtu, described the life of the royal family. For example, the daughters of Zimri-Lim and Shibtu sent letters to their mother and father that inform us about the different paths available to a princess.

    1. One daughter was a *naditum*, a woman who entered into the service of a god. These women usually were related to a king and would pray and perform rituals on behalf of the royal family.

2. At least three daughters were married to the rulers of cities nearby to cement alliances between these men and Zimri-Lim.

D. Among the surviving documents are records of the rations provided for nine female scribes, a rare piece of evidence for women engaged in this profession.

E. As noted earlier, other correspondence between Zimri-Lim and his generals also survives. Letters relating to his civil administration reveal some of the same problems that we've already described with Hammurabi.

F. The records also offer some illuminating evidence about nomads. Various tribes would camp near Mari for a few months at a time and interact with the people of Mari.

G. Smaller details also plagued Zimri-Lim. A curious letter describes the capture of a lion on the roof of a house; Zimri-Lim could expect it to arrive at the palace, confined in a cage, as a gift.

VI. The texts from Mari reveal the complicated diplomatic and military history of this era, as well as palace culture.

A. After Hammurabi attacked the city for the second time, this historical trading center effectively disappeared.

B. The letters preserved in the palace at Mari also show the many problems, such as questions of justice, that a king was called on to resolve.

Essential Reading:

Stephanie Dalley, *Mari and Karana: Two Old Babylonian Cities.*

Jean-Claude Margueron, "Mari: A Portrait in Art of a Mesopotamian City-State," in *CANE*, vol. II, pp. 885–900.

Supplementary Reading:

Wolfgang Heimpel, *Letters to the King of Mari.*

Questions to Consider:

1. What aspects of the letters from Mari are most surprising to you?

2. How are royal women involved in politics at this time?

Lecture Twenty-One—Transcript
Zimri-Lim of Mari

In the previous lecture, we discussed the reign of Hammurabi, who began as the ruler of the city-state of Babylon and he was not very powerful in the early part of his reign. He spent most of his time giving his attention to reinforcing the infrastructure of the state. Then, as he grew stronger, he led an army against the powerful states of Elam and Larsa. His success there created a large regional state that Hammurabi governed with the same attention to detail that he had given to Babylon earlier in his reign. If you recall, I did not describe the last major campaign that Hammurabi undertook against the rich state of Mari, in part, because there are so many sources for this era that I wanted to spend a little more time on this city. Another reason is that, during this attack, Mari was destroyed, ending the long history of this trading post. In this lecture, we will discuss the turbulent last few decades of Mari's history, in which it was controlled, first, by the Assyrians and then by its last ruler, Zimri-Lim.

The city of Mari was located on the northern Euphrates River in a position that controlled key trade routes between east and west. Mari was a very important power in the Early Dynastic period, which was about 2600–2300 B.C., but it is the city that dates to the 18th century that is best preserved. One reason for Mari's prosperity was that the city collected taxes on all goods that traveled between Syria and Mesopotamia along the Euphrates River. We've come to understand what sort of income this might provide in connection with the Old Assyrian traders. You remember that they pay taxes to the local rulers in order to try and protect their donkey caravans. The rulers had to ensure that these caravans would not be robbed along the way and, if so, they had to give the merchants some recompense for their loss.

In addition to the river trade, Mari was placed at a key point on the land route that crossed the desert from northern Mesopotamia to southern Syria. If you recall the number of times I've talked about trade between Mesopotamia and the west, Syria and Anatolia, you get a sense of how vibrant this trade was and what a longstanding part it was of the Mesopotamian economy. We have evidence for both diplomatic and military contacts between Mari and Mesopotamia from the Early Dynastic period until the time that

Hammurabi destroyed the city. You might recall that one of our early examples of gift exchange between rulers was found between the rulers of Ur and the rulers of Mari. That was about 2400 B.C. Military contacts are recorded during the Akkadian period, and both Sargon and Naram-Sin considered Mari an important target. And so, they referred to their attempts to control the city. They seem to have been unsuccessful, but it also reminds us that Mari remains a consistent object of desire for Mesopotamian rulers. An Amorite dynasty had taken control of Mari, just as they had in Babylonia, in the mid-19th century B.C.—so about 100 years before the period that we're going to discuss—and Mari was very prosperous during their reign. We determine this by the large building projects that can be dated to between the 19th and 18th centuries. We will look at the royal palace that we'll examine in more detail and also the irrigation projects that are recorded for this time. They also note that these irrigation canals greatly expanded the fertile land that was available to support the city.

In 1795 B.C., Mari was captured by Shamshi-Adad, the Assyrian ruler who ruled from 1808–1776. Shamshi-Adad, once he captured the throne of Ashur, this allowed him to expand and then dominate the northern Tigris River. Shamshi-Adad installed his younger son, Yasmah-Adad, on the throne in Mari; he put his older son on the throne in a city to the east, but Yasmah-Adad proved to be a very disappointing choice. Letters from Shamshi-Adad to his son reprimanded him for failing to organize his household and often would compare him unfavorably to his older brother. Shamshi-Adad wrote: "Don't you have a beard on your chin? When are you going to take charge of your house? Don't you see that your brother is leading vast armies? So you too, take charge of the palace!" Shamshi-Adad also made sure that his younger son knew of his brother's victories. "While your brother has won a great victory here, you remain there reclining among the women." They're not very good parenting skills. Yasmah-Adad responded to his father's denigration by complaining, "How can I be like a child and incapable of directing affairs when you, Daddy, promoted me?...I am coming to you right now to have it out with Daddy about my unhappiness." It doesn't seem that Yasmah-Adad actually did go face his father; he was living a very comfortable life in Mari. Even without these letters revealing the strained family dynamics of the Assyrian palace, Yasmah-Adad did not appear to have been an especially successful ruler and he disappeared from the throne of Mari almost immediately after his father's death. You might recall when we talked about food that I mentioned Yasmah-Adad as a king who was very concerned with getting the most exotic luxuries for his own personal meals.

Zimri-Lim became the new king of Mari in 1776 B.C. He claimed, probably falsely, that he had a blood relationship to the previous Amorite Dynasty and, since the Amorites had been so prosperous, this would help reinforce his claim to the throne. Whatever his origins, Zimri-Lim was a far better administrator than the Assyrian ruler Yasmah-Adad and the state of Mari was thriving economically while he was king. Politically, Zimri-Lim reestablished a strong diplomatic relationship with Babylon, and he also created a network of smaller vassal states that helped Mari expand. These diplomatic alliances were secured by marriages with Zimri-Lim's daughters and we'll come back to discuss those marriages a little bit later on. One reason for the focus on diplomacy rather than military expansion was that the king of Elam was still very powerful when Zimri-Lim took the throne. You will recall that the Elamite king would often arrange matters between the lesser kings of Mesopotamia, and basically everyone was a lesser king in comparison to him. Zimri-Lim was one of the rulers who fell under the Elamite king's control. That, too, gives us a sense of how strong this Elamite king was. He is in southwest Iran, Zimri-Lim is in northern Syria along the Euphrates, and yet Zimri-Lim considers himself a vassal and does what the king of Elam suggests.

One of the most contentious issues between Zimri-Lim and Hammurabi was the control over the city of Hit on the Euphrates. It was a little bit further south than Mari, right around the bend of the Euphrates. Both Hammurabi and Zimri-Lim desperately wanted control of Hit. Hammurabi wanted it because it was a source of bitumen, which is a binding caulk that is used in boats to make sure that they're waterproof. Hammurabi needed bitumen to build boats to transport his troops and also to ensure trade. One letter from Hammurabi to Zimri-Lim clarifies this need quite explicitly. Hammurabi writes: "Your country's power lies in donkeys and chariots. My country's power lies in ships. That is exactly why I really want the bitumen and pitch from that city. Why else would I want the city from him?" Perhaps, there would also be political reasons for having control over a city that far up the Euphrates, but Hammurabi really focuses on the bitumen as the source of his desire for Hit.

Zimri-Lim's interest in Hit was significantly different. Hit was the site of a judicial ritual called the river ordeal. Accused criminals would be taken to Hit and, once they arrived, they or some representative that they had chosen would have to survive a swimming challenge across the river. This was not just a set distance that the swimmer had to survive, that everyone had to cross, the challenge would be made significant; sometimes a swimmer would have to swim a very long distance underwater or sometimes they would have to swim with a millstone around their neck. So, this was quite the challenge. If the person completed the assigned task and survived, they were deemed innocent of whatever crime they had been brought to Hit in order to settle. Some of these crimes were adultery or theft—kind of basic crimes that we'll discuss in a later lecture on laws. If they did not survive, they would be deemed guilty, and so with this sort of challenge, you can imagine that many of them did not survive. It's hard to get a sense from the text how many could make it across the river. We do read records of swimmers who have been assigned to this challenge on a certain day—a woman died, a man survived, but we can't get a sense overall of how many would make it through.

After Hammurabi defeated the Elamites and he was the strongest ruler in Mesopotamia, the matter of Hit once again was the subject of debate between Hammurabi and Zimri-Lim. A letter to Zimri-Lim by one of his messengers reported one of Hammurabi's outbursts and this involved the matter of Hit. Hammurabi had just finished praising Zimri-Lim to his envoys—to Zimri-Lim's envoys—saying, "Among the allied kings there is indeed no one who has treated me as well and has honored me like Zimri-Lim. For all the good he has done for me, I will give him satisfaction and an eternal bond will be established between us." This initially very positive response from Hammurabi prompted the messengers to try to settle the matter of Hit, but Hammurabi immediately cut them off, saying, "Don't mention Hit." Hammurabi, instead, suggested that the two kings try to share power over this one city. As you can imagine, that probably wouldn't work out diplomatically. You'll also recall that Zimri-Lim had lent 2,000 troops to Hammurabi to help the Babylonian king defeat the Elamites. The slow return of these troops created more friction between Hammurabi and Zimri-Lim. Also, Hammurabi didn't respond quite as favorably as Zimri-Lim had done when Zimri-Lim tried to expand his power further west against some smaller rival states.

There was clearly an unequal relationship between the two kings and, as Hammurabi was gaining strength and becoming more powerful and more experienced as a military leader, the diplomatic situation between the two kings deteriorated. We don't know exactly what prompted Hammurabi to lead the attack against Mari, but we do have signs that Zimri-Lim was getting increasingly nervous about the Babylonian king's growing power. There were letters to his wife, Shibtu, asking for help interpreting oracles so that he could try to predict what Hammurabi would do. Shibtu comforted him by saying that she had consulted the oracles and they promised that Zimri-Lim would capture Hammurabi. In fact, there are several oracles recorded that were sent to Zimri-Lim stating quite positively that Zimri-Lim would defeat Hammurabi. In the end, Zimri-Lim was unable to overcome the Babylonian army. Hammurabi had sent two forces, they attacked from both the north and the south, and the city was captured in 1761.

The destruction of the city occurred two years after this initial attack. Again, we're not sure what prompted Hammurabi to take the next step. He already controlled the city; why did he then destroy it? We also have no idea what happened to Zimri-Lim; he disappeared after the attacks on the city were reported. The destruction of the city preserved its palace, which has been excavated by French archaeologists who began to explore the site in the 1930s. Archaeologists have uncovered much of the six-acre palace and the architecture is very well preserved, but it was largely emptied of its contents by Hammurabi's army. They would have looted the palace before they set fire to it and destroyed it. Zimri-Lim's palace was famous among the rulers of the Near East, as a letter from Hammurabi to Zimri-Lim—clearly in earlier, happier times—describes. Hammurabi writes: "To Zimri-Lim communicate the following from your brother Hammurabi. The king of Ugarit has written to me as follows: 'Show me the palace of Zimri-Lim! I wish to see it.' With this same courier I am sending on his man." Ugarit was a Syrian kingdom and the fame of Zimri-Lim's palace had reached the king of Ugarit and he wanted to explore its wonders; Hammurabi was negotiating this palace tour.

The palace had very thick walls—about five to nine yards thick—that surrounded it and the main entrance was through the north gate. This northern entrance drew visitors into a very large courtyard. The Mari texts refer to a courtyard as the "Court of Palms." So, it may have been here that palm trees were planted and so, as visitors would come in, they would enter this palm grove within the house of the king. It would have been lovely. There are 260 rooms in the palace complex and we have the same problems with identifying the purpose of different rooms that we have for domestic architecture on a much less grandiose scale. But, we can try to speculate based on the level of public versus private access, as well as the decoration of certain rooms. So, a room that was highly decorated with wall paintings, which are preserved at Mari, for example, might easily be conceived of as a reception room, where the king wants to show off his personal style. An example of these wall paintings—which are quite unusual because it's rare for wall paintings to be preserved. I've only talked about foundations in houses, so we don't have the walls on which the paintings would have been placed.

One example is found on the wall of a smaller courtyard that is deeper in the palace, beyond the supposed "Court of Palms." The painting has been called the "Investiture of Zimri-Lim" and it shows a male standing before the goddess Ishtar. She hands him a scepter, so the symbol of kingship. The style of the painting, which was painted over plaster that was laid on the mudbrick walls, is dated by art historians to shortly before the destruction of the palace, and so that is what creates the specific link with Zimri-Lim. We're not sure that he is the figure that is shown on the painting, but it's a good guess.

Sanctuaries and chapels to the gods were incorporated into the palace, and several statues of worshippers and deities of much less valuable material than Hammurabi's army would have taken have been left behind. One statue of a goddess made of limestone shows a standing figure. She's a little less than life-size and she holds a water jar in her hands, right in front of her. The water jar is tilted towards the viewer and we see that there's a hollow channel that would allow water to flow through the jar. And so, this is a little fountain that would have created a wonderful sound as visitors came into the room. This statue was placed in an antechamber supposedly to the throne room, and it may have been a little shrine to indicate the importance of water at Mari, as it is everywhere in Mesopotamia.

As you may have guessed, we have many records from the Mari palace, about 20,000 or so. These were preserved in archives that were fired in the final destruction. An interesting fact about these Mari archives is that we know Babylonian officials who occupied the palace went through Zimri-Lim's archives. They arranged them in boxes. They sent most of the letters from Hammurabi to Zimri-Lim back to Hammurabi, so they're lost; we only have a few of those surviving. Zimri-Lim's correspondence with other rulers in Syria and northern Mesopotamia could have provided valuable intelligence to Hammurabi, so they would have been sent back to him, as well. The rest of the palace archives were divided up by the Babylonians and they are labeled. That's how we know that it was Babylonian officials who organized the archives; we have the clay sealings, with their seal stone, and they have Babylonian names and also the year of Hammurabi's rule. Like Ama-Dugga, the palace housekeeper who refused to switch her allegiance from Yasmah-Adad to Zimri-Lim, these workers still called themselves the "servants of Zimri-Lim," so they may have been men who worked for Zimri-Lim, but under Hammurabi's rule, carried out his orders.

Letters from Zimri-Lim's wife and queen, Shibtu, described the life of the royal family. I mentioned the diplomatic alliances in marriages that Zimri-Lim's daughters were involved in. These daughters sent letters to their mother and father, and they explain the different paths that were available to a princess. One daughter was a *naditum*, which is a woman who entered into the service of a god. These women, when they appear in text, are often related to a king. They would pray and perform rituals on behalf of their family, so the king has special access to a goddess or a god through his daughter. The life of a royal naditum was quite comfortable and we read of gifts demanded by Zimri-Lim's daughter from her parents so that she can maintain her status, her way of life while she's still living in the temple. She sounds very spoiled. She wants a lot of gold. At least three daughters were married to the rulers of cities nearby and these would cement alliances between these men and Zimri-Lim. One daughter requested troops from her father on her husband's behalf, so that provides some insight into how a royal wife could negotiate on behalf of her husband. Another daughter was captured after her city was attacked and so that reveals the perils of the royal queen. A third was very unhappy in her marriage because she felt that her status was not being publicly displayed, that her husband was favoring a woman who was the daughter of another king over her, so she had a lot of complaints.

Among the surviving documents from the Mari archives, are rations provided for nine female scribes and this is a rare piece of evidence for women engaged in this profession. We'll see that Zimri-Lim seems to promote female professionals; he also had a female physician among his palace staff. Other correspondence between Zimri-Lim and his generals survives, and we've already discussed how they collected troops and conducted themselves in battle. The civil administration had many of the same problems that we've already described with Hammurabi. Zimri-Lim had to keep irrigation canals open and, even in the best of times, the territory around Mari couldn't grow enough food to support the population. So, Zimri-Lim had the added problem of making sure that there was open access to food supply. This wasn't usually a problem because remember Mari is located in such an important position for both land trade and river trade, but it does show us that kings had to use all of their resources to feed their people.

We also get some illuminating evidence for nomads; various tribes would encamp near Mari for a few months at a time and these tribes were very well known to the king. There's a close interaction between these groups that we don't normally get much evidence about and the people of Mari. Smaller details also plagued Zimri-Lim; a curious letter describes the capture of a lion on the roof of a house. The lion was being sent to Zimri-Lim in a wooden cage. This, presumably, was a present that Zimri-Lim would keep who knows where in his palace. I've always wondered what happened to the lion. You also might remember that it was Zimri-Lim who constructed the icehouse; we found that foundation stone that talks about how he created this new and impressive icehouse that would keep his drinks cool in the summer. Zimri-Lim also received truffles from a farmer. So, like his predecessor, Yasmah-Adad, Zimri-Lim had a very rich diet.

The texts from Mari demonstrate the very complicated diplomatic and military history of this era, as well as the palace culture. After

Hammurabi attacked the city for the second time, this historical trading center effectively disappears. We know that some people did live in the area after it was destroyed, but it never regained its prominence and its wealth as a link between northern and southern Mesopotamia, and also with Syria. We never know what happens to Zimri-Lim. He seems so worried and so beset by problems that it's hard not to feel sorry for him, in comparison to Hammurabi who has such a bad temper, he seems like a big bully. I've always felt very close to Zimri-Lim because of his anxiety and all of the problems that he had to worry about: his family life, whether his daughters were happy in marriage, whether his people had enough food, and what was Hammurabi doing. All of this kept him up at night and also kept him consulting oracles on a regular basis. This history of Mari also serves to remind us of the broader historical changes that are associated with Hammurabi's rule. Remember that it's under Hammurabi that we shift to large regional states; that meant it would be much more difficult for even a good ruler of a city-state like Zimri-Lim to withstand an opponent like Hammurabi. So, the big man who's at the head of a big army really starts to dominate our history at this point.

The letters preserved in the palace also show the many problems, such as questions of justice, that a king would resolve. All of these cases that required the intervention of the river ordeal to settle whether a person was guilty or innocent of adultery or any other property damage, or whatever the problem was, show that justice and settling legal disputes was an important role for the king. In the next lecture, we will examine several of the surviving law codes associated with kings—specifically, Hammurabi, which is probably the best known law code. We will see what matters were most contentious and how rulers in different eras tried to resolve them. Mostly, there would be fines enacted in order to settle the dispute. So, say a neighbor's wall fell down and damaged your house, then you would have to pay a fine. We'll also get some insight into the social organization of a city-state or regional state, and see that there are different levels of society and that the punishment varied according to your status in a particular city.

Lecture Twenty-Two
Laws

Scope:

Hammurabi is best known to history from the long list of laws attributed to him; in this respect, he followed a tradition of kings as dispensers of justice. In this lecture, we will survey the types of Mesopotamian laws that have survived, from the earliest laws dating to the very end of the 3rd millennium B.C., to Hammurabi's laws of the 18th century, to the 11th-century Middle Assyrian codes. First, we will survey the existing laws to consider the social ills they attempted to redress; then, we will examine the purpose of the law codes. Scholars increasingly see the term *law code* as anachronistic, misrepresenting both the purpose and the use of these law collections. A law code implies that the laws represent all the legal precepts in use at the time, but even the longest set of laws, that of Hammurabi, does not provide a comprehensive legal framework that could order a society. Finally, we will look at the Middle Assyrian precepts that regulated the appearance and behavior of the royal court, especially female courtiers.

Outline

I. The earliest collection of laws dates to the Ur III period (c. 2112–2004 B.C.) and consists of about 40 laws that address homicide, family issues, and personal injury.

    A. The laws are attributed either to Ur-Nammu, the founder of the Ur III dynasty, or to his son Shulgi; current opinion leans toward Ur-Nammu. The text includes a prologue that sets out the situation inherited by the king and outlines some of his tasks as ruler. Often, the king also lists the cities he governed.

    B. Ur-Nammu describes how he regulated trade and traffic on the rivers and highways, making them safe for his people and revealing an existing economic and social order.

    C. The first law of this code states, "If a man commits a homicide, they shall kill that man," followed by, "If a man acts lawlessly [word uncertain], they shall kill him."

D. The laws that follow are not presented in an obviously logical order.

E. Several of the laws concern women and marriage; for example, women who initiate sexual relations can be killed. When a man divorces his wife, he must hand over a mina of silver in compensation for turning her out of his house.

F. Personal injury laws established fines for damages done; fines were also levied against perjurers.

G. These laws reinforce the idea that kings are the mortal representatives of the gods, given the task of dispensing justice for their people.

H. Laws by other kings who followed Ur-Nammu survive in a fragmentary state, but they expand our comprehension of legal issues.

    1. When someone rents an ox and the animal is hurt, the renter pays fines that vary according to the severity of the animal's injury.

    2. If someone helps a slave escape or knowingly harbors an escaped slave, he must give up one of his slaves in compensation.

    3. If a neighbor cuts down one of your trees, he will pay you 20 shekels.

II. Hammurabi's law code is by far the most extensive legal text. It is engraved on a seven-foot basalt stele, now in the Louvre, that was recovered in Susa in Iran, where it had been taken as war booty about 500 years after Hammurabi's rule.

A. At the top of the monument is a scene carved in relief showing Hammurabi receiving his scepter from Shamash, the Sun god, the god of justice, and the patron deity of Sippar. The image provides visual corroboration of the god's approval of Hammurabi's rule.

B. The laws are engraved carefully in 49 columns. The text is divided into three sections: a prologue, the laws, and an epilogue.

C. Hammurabi first explains how the gods arranged themselves into a society and chose him as king to ensure justice. He then lists more than a dozen gods and cities that support him.

D. The first five laws are devoted to legal proceedings, specifically, legislation designed to prevent perjury and corrupt judges.

E. These laws are followed by penalties for property damage and theft, then problems that arise over real estate. Also addressed are matters concerned with loans, marriage and inheritance, fees for various professions, and rates for hiring workers, animals, or boats.

III. Certain themes recur in Hammurabi's law code.

A. One of the most informative aspects of the code relates to social status. The punishment for a crime usually varied according to the offender's status, and certain social classes were specifically defined in the laws.

    1. In Hammurabi's laws, three groups of people were listed: free people (*awilum*), slaves (*wardum*), and commoners (*mushkenum*).

    2. This seems to create a strict social framework, but in reality, these social classes raise additional questions.

B. As mentioned, penalties were connected to one's social status; for example, if a free person blinded another free person, then the offender would be blinded, but if a free person blinded a slave or commoner, he was to pay a fine.

    1. Although these distinctions in punishment may seem unjust, the fact that laws existed for each class ensured some level of protection, even for slaves.

    2. Most surviving laws provided for the poorest members of society and illustrated a desire to ensure justice for all.

C. In addition to social status, several laws referred to family connections and relationships. In general, the laws reinforced the authority of the father, who protected and controlled his family.

D. Several legal issues revolved around women and concerns specific to marriage and divorce.

    1. The divorce laws varied depending on whether the husband or the wife initiated the action. The price paid to a wife whose husband divorced her also varied depending on social status.

2. Reasons were also given for women to initiate divorce, such as abuse or adultery.

E. Inheritance laws provide further insight into family life and reveal an interest in protecting family property and preventing lawsuits between family members.

F. Laws were set forth to ensure that no one damaged irrigation canals or used them improperly.

    1. A negligent farmer who caused a flood by failing to reinforce the embankment on his section of a canal had to replace the lost grain.

    2. In contrast, a flood sent by the rain god Adad that resulted in a failed harvest would earn a debtor a year's reprieve on the interest of a loan.

G. The king also legislated fees and responsibilities for professions.

    1. Female innkeepers were singled out in two laws, one that required them to accept measures of grain as payment for beer in addition to silver and another that prevented them from allowing criminals to stay in their inns without reporting them to the palace. If an innkeeper failed to alert the authorities, she would be killed.

    2. Physicians' fees were established, with higher prices for surgery, especially eye surgery, than other aspects of healing. A physician could earn 10 shekels of silver for a successful operation on a free person's eye; if the surgery resulted in the death or blindness of the patient, then the surgeon's hand would be cut off.

    3. A veterinarian who operated on an ox or a donkey would be paid one sixth of a shekel if the animal was healed.

H. Architects and builders were held responsible for the safety of the structures they erected.

    1. If a builder constructed a house, but it was unsound and collapsed, killing the owner, then the builder would be killed; if the son of the homeowner was killed, then the builder's son would be killed.

    2. In less tragic circumstances, when no one died or was injured, the builder was required to repair the structure at his own expense.

3. Likewise, boatmen who lost cargo because of carelessness had to replace the goods.

I. Hammurabi concluded his list of laws with a praise poem to himself and a message to future kings. Should a future ruler contemplate changing Hammurabi's laws, the Babylonian king encourages the gods to visit terrible ordeals on him.

IV. Although Hammurabi's laws seem extensive, they do not address many important social ills nor do they create a workable set of legal precedents that could effectively resolve disputes.

A. A survey of all law codes shows that the laws were not always new but could belong to earlier codes issued by other kings. Further, major components of a well-established legal system are missing; the basic organization of a justice system, along with civic and political responsibilities, is not established in these texts.

B. The goal of a law code likely was not practical but ideological. Through a law code, the king guarantees justice, and the fact that he displays these laws in public proves his concern for justice.

C. If we view the law codes as part of a king's message to his people, we see that rulers had to acknowledge different economic and social distinctions to show their willingness to protect all members of society.

V. A final group of laws from Mesopotamia is not nearly as well known as Hammurabi's code but shows major shifts in one area of Mesopotamian society that we have discussed several times—the position and status of women.

A. These laws from the Middle Assyrian period address situations in which women figure prominently, as victims or instigators of a crime. The punishments mandated in these laws often included bodily mutilation; a woman who stole, for example, could have her ears cut off by her husband. Death is mandated for any woman who commits adultery.

B. Another group of edicts governs the behavior of palace officials, especially women. The goal here was to control interactions between men and women. Usually, men and women were separated into different quarters of the palace, and a man had to have permission to visit the women's quarters. Eunuchs were employed in the palace, but the regulations permit eunuchs to speak to women only with permission of the palace commander.

C. These laws mandate that women be veiled and have their shoulders covered in any conversation with a male attendant. Even conversational distance between males and females was established—no closer than seven paces.

D. These Middle Assyrian laws seem much more restrictive than laws of the earlier periods we have discussed, especially with respect to women.

VI. Laws are fascinating for the specific situations or issues they describe and the manner in which rulers settled them.

A. From law codes, we can determine the issues that were probably the most contentious, such as property disputes, especially with respect to inheritance or divorce, or those that required an intermediary, such as setting wages and fees, as well as penalties. Social divisions required different levels of punishment, as did one's gender.

B. We can't know how these laws were enforced in Babylon or Ashur; for example, we have evidence for lawsuits and corrupt judges, but nothing about lawyers or advocates. Law codes were, in reality, another public monument sponsored by the king to promote his rule to his subjects.

C. In the next lecture, we move from the laws set by kings to a survey of the scientific fields that attracted the curiosity of the Babylonians.

Essential Reading:

Martha T. Roth, *Law Collections from Mesopotamia and Asia Minor*.

Elizabeth M. Tetlow, *Women, Crime and Punishment in Ancient Law and Society: Ancient Mesopotamia*.

Questions to Consider:

1. What issues seem to be most pressing in Mesopotamian collections of laws? How do they help to inform us about social tensions?

2. If these laws are intended to represent the concern of the king for justice, how should that affect our interpretation?

Lecture Twenty-Two—Transcript
Laws

Hammurabi is best known to history from the long list of laws attributed to him. In this respect, he follows a tradition of kings as dispensers of justice. In this lecture, we will survey the types of Mesopotamian law that have survived, from the earliest laws dating to the very end of the 3rd millennium B.C., to Hammurabi's laws of the 18th century, and finally, to the 11th-century Middle Assyrian codes and edicts.

First, we will look at the laws that survive to get a sense of the social ills that they attempted to redress and then we will consider what the purpose of the law codes was. This probably seems obvious, but in fact, scholars increasingly see the term law code as anachronistic and a misrepresentation both of the purpose and the use of these law collections. A law code implies that the laws represent all of the legal precepts that are in use at the time, but even the longest set of laws, that of Hammurabi—over 200—does not provide a comprehensive legal framework that could really order a society. Finally, we will look at the Middle Assyrian precepts that regulated the appearance and behavior of the royal court, especially female courtiers. These are sort of different type of laws, but they're very interesting because they show a distinct shift in how women are supposed to behave.

The earliest collection of laws dates to the Ur III period and remember that was from 2112–2004 B.C. It's a list of about 40 laws that address homicide, family issues, and personal injury. The laws are assigned to Ur-Nammu, the founder of the dynasty, or to Shulgi, his son who followed him. Currently, scholars lean towards assigning the laws to Ur-Nammu, so we will follow that assumption. The text includes a prologue, which is a very common feature of Mesopotamian law codes, and this prologue is focused on the king. It sets out the situation of the king, mostly focused on which gods approved him and also his tasks as ruler, so they're very repetitive. We've gotten pretty used to the idea of what a king does, but the prologue can also list the cities or regions that a king governed. They can be very useful for helping us assign a date to the law code and we know when the law code was sent out in the reign of a king.

Ur-Nammu describes how he regulated trade and traffic on the rivers and highways in his prologue and he made them safe for his people.

He also writes that, "I did not deliver the orphan to the rich. I did not deliver the widow to the mighty. I did not deliver the man with one shekel to the man with one mina. I did not deliver the man with but one sheep to the man with one ox." This phrase sets out an economic and social order that is present in our earliest surviving law code. Ur-Nammu continues that, "I eliminated enmity, violence and cries for justice. I established justice in the land." So, this is the purpose of his law code, to show that he is overseeing all of the needs of his people, and he concludes with a focus on justice, without which the rest of society can't really run effectively.

With this prologue, I am sure you are ready to hear what the first law is, and indeed, the fist law states: "If a man commits a homicide, they shall kill that man." It's followed by, "If a man acts lawlessly"—and the word here is uncertain—"they shall kill him." We would really like to know the meaning of that specific word, what does lawlessly mean, since it incurs such a harsh judgment. After these first two laws, there is not necessarily a logical order to the laws that follow. For example, the fourth law concerns marriage between slaves and it would not seem to be as pressing as laws concerning homicide.

Several of the laws are devoted to women and marriage. Women who initiate sexual relations can be killed; men who divorce their wives must give compensation to them. In Ur-Nammu's laws, they must compensate their wives with one mina of silver if he is going to turn her out of his house. Personal-injury laws establish fines for the damage done and fines were also levied against perjurers. There's an indication in these laws that the legal system must be kept pure. It cannot be corrupted. All of these laws combine to reinforce the idea that the kings are the representatives of gods on earth. They are given the task of making sure that the people have a fair and just legal system.

Laws by other kings, who followed Ur-Nammu, survive in a fragmentary state and they expand our comprehension of legal issues. What happens when someone rents an ox and the animal is hurt? They pay fines that vary according to the severity of the animal's injury. Can someone help a slave escape or knowingly harbor an escaped slave? Not unless they want to give up one of their own slaves in compensation for this. If a neighbor cuts down one of the trees in your date orchard that you've been cultivating for years, he has to pay you 20 shekels in recompense for this damage he's done to your property.

Hammurabi's law code is by far the most extensive and it was engraved on a basalt stele now in the Louvre. This stele was recovered not anywhere in Hammurabi's kingdom, but in Susa in Iran, where it had been taken as loot by soldiers about 500 years after Hammurabi's rule. We discussed other monuments that were taken in this raid, as well. The Stele of Hammurabi is over seven feet tall and, at the top, is a scene carved in relief showing Hammurabi approaching the god Shamash. Shamash is the sun god and he is also the god of justice. You can imagine that the sun god who can see everything and who shines so brightly would be very naturally linked with justice. Shamash is also the patron deity of Sippar and it's possible that Hammurabi's law code was originally displayed in Sippar, so that's why he is shown specifically with this deity. Hammurabi receives a scepter from Shamash who is seated before him and this is very much like Zimri-Lim's painting at Mari showing the investiture of the king—that the gods are physically handing over the symbol of kingship to the ruler. This scene provides a visual corroboration of the god's approval of Hammurabi's rule and, implicitly, their approval of the justice system that he is about to set out.

The laws are engraved in 49 columns and they are beautifully engraved. This is some of the most beautiful cuneiform that you'll ever see, very even and straight. The code itself is divided into three parts: a prologue, the laws, and then an epilogue. Hammurabi first explains how the gods arranged themselves into a society and that they decreed for the "well being of the people, [the gods] named me by my name, Hammurabi, the pious prince, who venerates the gods, to make justice prevail in the land." Hammurabi then lists over a dozen gods who are the patron deities of cities that support him and from this we know that the law code dates to the latter part of his reign when he had control over a lot of territory.

The first five laws of Hammurabi's code are devoted to legal proceedings, specifically legislation that is designed to prevent perjury and corrupt judges. "If a man accuses another man and charges him with homicide but cannot bring proof against him, his accuser shall be killed." The laws that follow include penalties for property damage, theft, and then issues that crop over real estate—

say, not maintaining one's section of an irrigation canal or controlling animals that inflict damage on your property. Hammurabi then is concerned with matters of loans. There is a large section devoted to marriage and inheritance, and this section makes up the majority of the laws. What follows provides very specific information about the fees for various professions and the rates that could be set to hire animals or workers or even boats or other sorts of equipment that one would need to conduct one's business.

As we look more closely at Hammurabi's laws, we'll focus on a few themes. One of the most informative aspects of Hammurabi's law code relates to social status, since the punishment for a crime usually varied according to one's status. Certain social classes were defined in these laws. Hammurabi's laws set out three groups of people: the free person, who is called an *awilum*, a slave, who is called a *wardum*, and commoners, who are called *mushkenum*. This leaves a lot of room for people in between. If someone is not a free person or a slave, what does this status of commoner mean? We're very uncertain about who these people were. Even though we see what seems to be a very strict framework with punishments connected to what your status in society is, in reality, these social classes raise more questions and this is indicative of the laws as a whole, as we'll see. From what we can tell, the last group of commoners did not merit all of the rights of free men and women, but they were not owned as slaves were. They were somewhere in between and we'd like to know exactly what their connection was that meant that they owed something to some individual that made them of a lesser status than a freed person.

If a free person blinded another free person or an *awilum*, then the offender would be blinded. But, if a free person blinded a slave or commoner, he then had to pay a fine for this crime. Although these distinctions in punishment may seem unjust, the fact that laws existed for each class ensured some level of protection, even for the slave. Most surviving laws provide for the poorest members of society and this illustrates a desire to provide justice for all. So, just as a king provides work for widows and orphans and he gives them food and compensation for this work, the laws, too, are focused on the poorest members of society and give them some protection.

In addition to social status, several laws refer to family connections and relationships, and these are the marriage laws that I referred to earlier. In general, the laws reinforced the authority of the father or the husband. The father both protected and controlled his family. The laws of Hammurabi go so far as to give fathers permission to cut off the hand of a son who struck him. This seems very extreme and it's also unlikely that this type of penalty would be carried out very often, but they do demonstrate the level of legal control that the fathers had over their families. This control would be guaranteed by the king, so it does show that this is a very paternalistic society.

Several legal issues revolved around women and concerns specific to marriage and divorce. The divorce laws vary, depending on whether the husband or the wife initiates the process. Hammurabi writes: "If a man intends to divorce his first-ranking wife who did not bear him children, he shall give her one mina of silver and restore to her the dowry that she brought from her father's house and he shall divorce her." Again, the price that a husband would pay depended on his status. So, a commoner or *mushkenum* would pay 20 shekels of silver instead of 1 mina of silver.

Some reasons are also provided in these laws for women to divorce. One law describes a woman who began divorce proceedings because her husband has been wayward and verbally abusive. Once she levied this charge against him, then the authorities of the city would investigate. So, already, we see a distinction between a husband beginning a divorce and a wife beginning a divorce. The husband simply has to cough up some money and the divorce is final. A wife has to have outside authorities verify that her charge is correct. If they do find that her account is valid, then she can take her dowry and divorce her husband, returning to her father's house. She will not get an additional amount of money to support her if she begins the divorce, but she does receive her dowry. Also, notice that she is supposed to go right back to her father's house, so she is under the control of some male member of society. When we talked about the widows at Nuzi who seemed to be so powerful, I noted that they were somewhat unusual, and the laws of Hammurabi and other legal codes also reinforced the idea that women were supposed to be connected to a male authority—either a father or a husband. Laws indicate that men rarely had to provide a just cause for a divorce. Even though divorce is a common theme in the law codes that survive from Mesopotamia, it's hard for us to know how common it was. It's something that concerns kings who want to make sure that property is divided fairly, but we don't have any sense, even from other texts, of how common divorce would be.

Inheritance laws also provide insight into family life. If a man has children by his wife and by a slave, according to Hammurabi's law code, and he acknowledges the paternity of the slave's children while he's still alive, the children by both women can inherit equally. If he does not claim the slave's children as his while he's alive, they will not inherit anything. So, the issue of paternity must be settled by the father. Family issues could be very complex and there is a lot of interest in trying to protect family property and trying to prevent lawsuits between different members of the family.

As we move from looking at the family to broader issues that Hammurabi was concerned with, we'll see that it's not surprising that a king who was responsible for irrigation canals also ensured that no one damaged them or used them improperly. A negligent farmer who did not maintain his section of a canal—and they would do this by reinforcing the embankment to make sure that the water didn't come over the boundary—if the canal flooded a neighbor's field, the person who had not maintained his part of the canal had to replace the lost grain. Natural disasters are also acknowledged. A flood sent by the rain god Adad that resulted in a failed harvest would earn a debtor a year's reprieve on the interest of a loan.

The king also legislated the fees and responsibilities of specific professions. We don't have the entire range of professions by any means and just at a look at few examples will show how specific these are. Female innkeepers are singled out in two laws of Hammurabi; one required her to accept measures of grain as payment for beer, in addition to silver, and another prevents her from allowing criminals to stay in her inn without reporting them to the palace. If she does so—and we don't know if the same punishment will be inflicted if she harbors criminals knowingly or unknowingly—but if criminals are discovered and she has not reported them to the palace, she will be killed. Here we have a focus on female innkeepers, but nowhere do we have male innkeepers in Hammurabi's laws. We see that there's kind of an unusual perspective on professional life in Mesopotamia.

Physicians' fees were established and there were higher prices for surgery, especially eye surgery, than other aspects of healing. A surgeon could earn 10 shekels of silver for a successful operation on a free person's eye. If the surgery resulted in the death or blindness of the patient, then the surgeon's hand would be cut off—a harsh penalty. Veterinarians who operated on an ox or a donkey would be paid one-sixth of a shekel, if the animal was healed. If it was not healed, then the veterinarian would have to pay a fine to the owner, so it makes you wonder why anyone would want to go into the healing profession in antiquity.

Architects and builders were held responsible for the safety of the structures that they constructed. If a builder built a house and it was unsound and collapsed, killing the owner, the builder would be killed. If the homeowner's son had been killed, then the builder's son was killed. There's a very equal retribution, and these would all be for free persons. In less tragic circumstances when no one died or was injured, then the builder was required to repair the house at his own expense. Likewise, boatmen who lost cargo because of their carelessness in transporting the load up or down the river had to replace the goods at their own expense. So, we see that if you were engaged in certain professions, you had responsibilities to your customers.

Hammurabi concluded his list of laws with a praise poem to himself and a message to future kings. He urged his successors to "observe the pronouncements of justice that I have inscribed on my stele" and to not "alter the judgments that I rendered and the verdicts that I gave, nor remove my engraved image." Should a future ruler even contemplate changing Hammurabi's laws, the Babylonian king encouraged the gods to visit terrible ordeals on him—illness inflicted on his own body and famine and devastation throughout his lands.

Although Hammurabi's laws seem extensive and even very specific, they do not address many important social ills, nor do they create a workable set of legal precedents that could effectively resolve disputes. We have only one text from all of Mesopotamian literature that even refers to the concept of legal precedent. So, this fundamental aspect of laws and a legal system did not seem to exist in Mesopotamia. These gaps in the laws lead us to think that the law codes had a different purpose than what we would imagine them to have simply by reading the lists of laws. A survey of all of the law codes shows that the laws preserved were not always new, so a king did not establish a new set of laws when he came to the throne. There are also major components of a well-established legal system that are missing from these law codes. So, we don't have any idea of the basic organization of the justice system, or civic or political responsibilities of the king of the city; these would be important if a king wants to ensure justice throughout his land.

The goal of the law code was not practical, but instead was ideological. The king guarantees justice. He looks at all of the laws, all of the people he protects, and the fact that he displays these laws in public proves his concern for justice. We know, for example, for Hammurabi's law code, that many other copies were set up throughout the kingdom and that is the important purpose of these law codes. They are visible and present for people to see. They remind them that the king cares about justice. We've also referred to Hammurabi's legacy in a previous lecture and the laws that he created were copied for centuries. This shows that his legal code was an important part of his legacy and he was remembered for them. Later kings will refer to themselves as being someone who is as concerned for justice as Hammurabi was, for example. If we think of the law codes as part of the king's message to his people rather than a set of specific of laws, it gives us a very different way of thinking about them. I think it's even more intriguing than looking at the remnants of a legal system because it shows that the king has to acknowledge many different levels of society. And so, he demonstrates to his people that he's aware of economic and social distinctions, and he will provide a law that protects them no matter what it is.

A final group of laws from Mesopotamia is not nearly as well known as Hammurabi's, but they show a major shift in one aspect of Mesopotamian society that we have discussed several times—the status of women. The laws provide for situations in which women figure prominently, either as victims or instigators of a crime. The punishment mandated in these laws often included bodily mutilation. A woman who stole could have her ears cut off by her husband. Death is mandated for any woman who commits adultery and this is not specific to the middle Assyrian laws that are so concerned with women, but the scenarios in which a woman commits adultery and the effects of her punishment are described quite explicitly. It's a little gruesome to imagine all of these women with ears cut off, noses cut off, and other body parts that are damaged, and then she can be killed for seemingly looking at another man.

Another group of edicts from the middle Assyrian period governs the behavior of palace officials, especially the women. The goal here was to control interaction between men and women. Usually, men and women would be separated into different quarters of the palace and any man who had to visit the women's quarters must receive permission from certain officials in order to approach them. Eunuchs were widely employed in the palace and they were most often the messengers that would be sent to the women's quarters, but even eunuchs had to follow very specific and strict regulations. They could only speak to women with the permission of the palace commander. The king also ordered that women be veiled and have their shoulders covered in any conversation with a male attendant. Even the distance between the male and the female was set out; no one should be closer than seven paces from a member of the opposite sex for any conversation, otherwise this would raise the suspicion of those who were watching them.

Middle Assyrian society appears to be much more restrictive than the earlier periods that we have been talking about, especially with respect to women. This may reflect the specific culture of the palace; a king would be specifically worried about questions of legitimacy for his children than occurred in the rest of the kingdom. But, the change is so obvious and seems so severe and strict that it's hard not to imagine that the rest of middle Assyrian society was equally regulated and ordered.

The laws that we've seen are fascinating for the very specific situations that they describe and the manners in which rulers settled them. The laws show the areas that were probably the most litigious: property issues, especially with respect to inheritance or divorce, or issues that required an intermediary, such as a higher authority setting wages and fees, as well as penalties for various crimes. Social divisions required different levels of punishment. There is also a sense of gender inequity; overall, a woman's movements and her behavior are more highly suspected than any behavior of a male.

We can't know how these laws were enacted in Babylon or Ashur; nothing in the code explains how the whole legal system works. We hear lots about lawsuits and corrupt judges, but nothing about lawyers or advocates. So, who was involved in these lawsuits? Was it only the two individuals who were quarreling? Law codes, as they have become known, were, in reality, yet another type of public monument sponsored by the king to promote his rule to his subjects and to ensure his legacy in the future.

In the next lecture, we will move from the laws set by kings to a survey of the scientific fields that attracted the curiosity of the Babylonians.

Lecture Twenty-Three
Medicine, Science, and Math

Scope:

In this lecture, we will examine scientific thought and how science helped to order and explain the natural world for Mesopotamian cultures. We will discuss medicine, mathematics, astronomy, and divination, which in the world of Mesopotamia, was the most challenging and important science. Certain scientific achievements, especially Babylonian astronomy, enhanced the fame of the region in antiquity, but others, such as medicine, were mocked. In an otherwise admiring description of Babylon, Herodotus, a 5th-century B.C. Greek historian, dismissed the entire field of Babylonian medicine. He claimed that the Babylonians had no use for physicians and that if someone fell sick, he would be taken to the marketplace, where everyone who walked by spoke to the sufferer, giving advice or comfort. As we will see, this assessment of Babylonian medicine was quite inaccurate.

Outline

I. Evidence about the practice of medicine in Mesopotamia comes from lists of symptoms and their treatment, prescriptions, and some clues from law codes, but most of the texts we have were created by scribes practicing signs, not from practical handbooks used by physicians.

A. The practice of medicine involved a combination of magic and diagnostic skill to successfully treat illness, because disease was seen as a struggle between good and evil.

B. All sickness and suffering was inflicted by demons. Sometimes, the demons did this without motive, but sometimes, illness came as the result of an evil act by an individual or a family member. Ancient medical texts list both the affliction and its cause.

C. Because illness represented a moral deficiency and a physical malady, it required specialists in both fields. An *ashipu* was a priest or diviner, who was consulted to determine the cause of the evil and to cast spells to drive out the demon.

1. A group of texts was devoted to helping the *ashipu* understand the meaning of omens that he saw on the way to a patient's home. Most of these were fairly pessimistic. For example, if an *ashipu* saw a black pig, the patient would die; if he saw a white pig, the patient would be cured or he would be in great distress.

2. In addition to casting spells to drive out demons, the *ashipu* made amulets to help protect individuals from the curse of illness.

II. Even though sickness was a manifestation of evil, it also needed to be treated by a physician, called an *asu*.

A. Diagnosis required the rational observation of symptoms to undertake the correct treatment; this aspect of Babylonian medicine indicates a scientific approach. A physician would examine the patient, check his or her temperature all over the body, and look for discoloration or inflammation of the skin.

B. Several medical texts detail particular types of ailments. Gynecological problems and skin and eye diseases were especially common in the written sources. An entry describing an illness consisted of two parts, first, a description of the symptoms and, second, the treatment or, occasionally, the prognosis.

C. Prescriptions were made by combining plants and herbs with minerals or animal products.

D. Medicine was delivered in pill form; added to beer, wine, or water; and inhaled in steam baths. Plasters and salves could be applied topically. Some remedies, such as potassium nitrate, are still used today.

E. The concept of contagion was known in Mesopotamian medicine, but the causes were not understood.

F. Kings had their own physicians; sometimes, if a fellow ruler fell ill, another king would send his court physician to help effect a cure. Zimri-Lim listed a female physician among his staff, and a few other female physicians are known; midwives also commonly appear in texts.

G. Surgeons are known, as well, although rarely from medical texts. Instead, they are described in legal texts that assign fines when a surgeon fails or protects the surgeon from malpractice lawsuits.

H. Our study of Babylonian medicine is hindered by the fact that most subjects were learned through hands-on experience rather than from texts. Thus, it is difficult know important details about this subject.

III. A good knowledge of mathematics was a necessity in all periods in order to keep accurate records in the royal and temple bureaucracies.

A. Weights and measurements were standardized at regular intervals. Often, multiple systems of weights and measures were used simultaneously by traders from different nations.

B. In addition to accounting records, tablets show work with multiplication tables, division, reciprocals, and square roots. More complex problems, usually involving algebra rather than geometry, and word problems were computed, as well. These problems focused on specific cases and did not establish general formulations or proofs.

    1. Sometimes, the method of reckoning the answer for a problem is provided, indicating that an experienced mathematician had set out the problem. Often, however, only the solution is shown, making it seem as if the problem was part of a dictation or practice exercise.

    2. The tablets show little interest on the part of the recorder in divining whether the answer was exactly right or approximate.

    3. Other mathematical concepts, such as the properties of triangles, circles, and rectangles, were known, but there was not much interest in discovering the more complex properties of surface area and volume of these figures.

C. Mesopotamian mathematics used a place-value system based on units of 60 (sexagesimal), in which the meaning of a number depends on its position relative to other numbers. Babylonian mathematics was the only ancient system that developed this method, still in use today.

D. The concept of zero did not exist until the 8th century B.C., which caused difficulties for Babylonian mathematicians.

E. Most of the evidence for mathematics comes from word

problems, probably because these texts were used in scribal schools.

IV. Turning to science, astronomy was the field in which the most precise evidence was collected. Kings and priests were especially interested in any science that allowed them to predict the future or to interpret omens, and this aspect of the science connects astronomy with the practice of divination.

   A. Divination was one of the most important scientific disciplines developed in Mesopotamia and the one that would have helped make sense of the world.

   B. Divination revealed the gods' communication regarding the destiny of individuals. It required the belief that the natural world had the potential to reveal future events; diviners had to master many different skills to interpret signs.

   1. For example, animal entrails, especially livers, could be studied and interpreted; this practice is found in other cultures, as well.

   2. Other techniques, such as interpreting the patterns of oil poured over water or how smoke rose from incense, were used by experts to try to find answers to questions.

   3. Observations of animal behavior, such as how an animal approached the gates of a city or the altar of a temple, or the birth of a cow with specific markings could also portend the future.

   C. Special purification rituals could prevent or weaken the effects of a bad omen; in other words, diviners could attempt to change the future.

   D. We are best informed about divination through celestial observations.

   1. The Babylonian Astronomical Diaries are records of observations that astronomers in Babylon undertook from the Esagila, the temple of Marduk.

   2. The diaries note events that occurred night or day in the sky, as well as changes in the weather or the depth of the river. These diaries are preserved from the 7th century B.C. on, although they are often in fragments.

   E. The Persians, who succeeded the Babylonians, were also known for their interest in astronomy.

1. The Babylonians created a lunar calendar based on a 19-year interval. For 12 years, the year had 12 months; then for 7 years, the year had 13 months, for a total of 235 months.
2. Some of the observations that survive are focused on the appearance of a new moon and offer predictions about how the moon will affect the future.
3. Natural phenomena, such as earthquakes, were especially troubling.
4. Long lists of these descriptions and interpretations exist to help future diviners understand the meaning of events; these lists also give us a sort of natural history.

F. One of the most valuable achievements in astronomy could have been the ability to predict eclipses.

1. The records of these eclipses help modern scholars reconstruct a chronology for Mesopotamian history.
2. Unfortunately, there are three possible years for most of these events; thus, we remain uncertain about the exact year in which specific events occurred.

V. Much of the evidence for Mesopotamian scientific thought and literature was found in the library of the 7th-century B.C. Assyrian ruler Ashurbanipal at Nineveh.

A. More than 25,000 tablets were found in the palace of Ashurbanipal; about half of these were scientific or literary compositions. These tablets form the bulk of evidence from which we derive our knowledge of medicine, astronomy, and mathematics.

B. Several letters from Ashurbanipal note his interest in amassing tablets, and his collection from Nineveh is the largest single library of tablets from Mesopotamia. It preserves many of the texts we have discussed in this lecture and the most complete versions of the Gilgamesh epic.

C. A *colophon*, which is a heading that usually gives the first line of a poem, for example, or describes what the text is about, was added to many of the manuscripts that scribes copied for the library in Nineveh. Some noted that the text had been collected by Ashurbanipal; others were lengthier.

D. One reason for Ashurbanipal's obsession with collecting

texts is that he was controlling access to information that could explain the future through science. Further, he was interested in creating a legacy for successive rulers.

Essential Reading:

Francesca Rochberg, "Astronomy and Calendars in Ancient Mesopotamia," in *CANE,* vol. III, pp. 1925–1940.

Marvin Powell, "Metrology and Mathematics in Ancient Mesopotamia," in *CANE*, vol. III, pp. 1941–1958.

Robert D. Biggs, "Medicine, Surgery and Public Health in Ancient Mesopotamia," in *CANE*, vol. III, pp. 1911–1924.

Questions to Consider:

1. In what ways do science and religion interact in Mesopotamian thought?

2. What were the goals of these scientific disciplines?

Lecture Twenty-Three—Transcript
Medicine, Science, and Math

Our study of Mesopotamian law centered on the organization of society and the role of the king in the justice system. As we looked at laws, we examined the different social levels that created a hierarchy. In this lecture, we will study scientific thought and how science helped to order and explain the natural world for Mesopotamian cultures. We will discuss medicine, math, astronomy, and divination, which in the world of Mesopotamia, was considered the most challenging and important science.

Certain scientific achievements, especially Babylonian astronomy, enhanced the fame of the region in antiquity, but others, like medicine, were mocked. In an otherwise admiring description of Babylon, Herodotus, a 5th-century B.C. Greek historian, dismissed the entire field of Babylonian medicine. He claimed that they had no use for physicians and that if someone fell sick, they would be taken to the marketplace where everyone who walked by had to speak to the sufferer, giving advice if they had suffered a similar illness or comforting the person if they had nothing positive to convey—sort of like a broken down car with a bunch of mechanics looking at it. We'll see that this is quite inaccurate and that, in fact, medicine required a significant consultation with physicians and other healers.

Our evidence for medicine comes from lists of symptoms and their treatment. These lists are preserved on tablets that arrange the illnesses from head to toe, so it's a very orderly arrangement of illness, also prescriptions. We get some clues about the role of the physician from laws, such as Hammurabi's law code, which we discussed in the previous lecture. Most of these texts were created by scribes used to teach them to practice signs and symbols; they are not to be understood as handbooks that physicians actually consulted. What we're seeing is what scribes thought physicians did, rather than a description of what physicians actually did. Most physicians would have learned their trade from experience, presumably shadowing another doctor.

One of the first concepts that we have to grapple with is that the practice of medicine in Mesopotamia involved a combination of magic and diagnostic skill to successfully treat illness. Disease was considered a struggle between good and evil. In Mesopotamian thought, all sickness and suffering was inflicted by demons. Sometimes these demons did it without motive, so they're sort of mischief-makers. But, sometimes, illness came as the result of an evil act either by the person who was sick or perhaps a family member. So, you can imagine that it's very difficult to try and work out what the source of evil was that caused you to have this fever. We see this combination of both magic and, what we would consider, more practical medicine in the medical texts, which list the affliction and the cause. One text writes: "If the patient keeps crying, 'My skull, my skull!' it is the hand of the god." So, the gods are physically involved in inflicting pain on their people.

Since illness was represented as a moral deficiency and a physical malady, it required specialists in both fields. An *ashipu* was a priest or diviner, who was consulted to try and determine the cause of the evil and to cast spells to drive out the demon that was causing the illness. A group of texts devoted to helping the ashipu understand the meaning of omens that he might see on the way to a patient's house clarifies this. Most of the omens are pretty pessimistic and it does not look good for the patient. For example, if an ashipu saw a black pig, the patient would die; if he saw a white pig, the patient would be cured or he would be in great distress. There are other signs that an ashipu could see; it's not just focused on pigs. But, you can see that even as the ashipu travels to help the sick individual, that the illness can be exacerbated or lessened depending on what happens on his way to the house.

In addition to casting spells to drive out demons, an ashipu could make amulets to help protect individuals from the curse of an illness, so this is a sort of preventive medicine. While illness was a manifestation of evil, it also needed to be treated by a physician who was called an *asu*. The diagnosis of illness required the rational observation of symptoms in order to undertake the correct treatment, and this shows the scientific approach of Babylonian medicine. A physician would examine the patient, check their temperature all over their body, and look for any discoloration or inflammation of the skin. This would be what he would do immediately upon arrival. Several medical texts detail particular types of ailment. Gynecological problems and skin and eye diseases were especially common in the written sources. An entry describing an illness would consist of two parts; the first was a description of the symptoms and the second was the treatment, or occasionally the prognosis. Just as we saw with the ashipu and the omens that he could see on the way to the patient's home, the prognosis is often not good. One example of this is a list that includes the description of a stroke. "If a man is stricken with a stroke of the face and his whole torso feels paralyzed…he will die."

Prescriptions were made by combining plants and herbs with minerals or animal products. We don't know the exact recipe used for these prescriptions because the names of some of the plants can't be correlated with known flora or fauna. So, we don't know what exactly the physician was using as he was creating this prescription. We do know that prescriptions were delivered in pill form and they could be added to beer, wine, or water. Sometimes they were even inhaled in steam baths. Plaster and skin salves could be applied topically either over or under bandages. And, some remedies, such as potassium nitrate, are still used today.

The concept of contagion was known in Mesopotamian medicine, but the causes weren't really understood. Our evidence for this knowledge comes from our old friend Zimri-Lim who advised his wife to avoid a woman in her quarters who was sick and this would prevent her from being ill. Kings had their own physicians and, sometimes, if a fellow ruler fell ill, they would send their court physician to help affect a cure. The king, of course, would have the best-known physicians and the most successful doctors to help him survive illness. Zimri-Lim listed a female physician among his staff, and a few female physicians—even surgeons—are known. But, midwives appear much more commonly in texts. Some of the texts in which midwives appear are songs or spells that would be chanted during childbirth to help ease the delivery or prevent illness of either the child or the mother. Midwives are constantly referred to in these texts. Surgeons are also known, although rarely from medical texts. We've seen this already in the law code of Hammurabi that assigned a fine or a punishment when a surgeon fails to perform his task successfully. A few laws also protected the surgeon from malpractice lawsuits. The study of medicine is hindered by the fact that most subjects were learned through hands-on experience rather than from texts. Doctors didn't go to school where they learned how to read or write and read the list of symptoms that I've been describing, so it is difficult to know even the important details about this subject.

As we move from medicine to mathematics, we should suspect, just from our discussion of Mesopotamian culture, that a good knowledge of mathematics was necessary in all periods. We've seen a lot of records that record rations that were distributed, and so both the royal and the temple bureaucracy would need to have scribes that were familiar with accounting. Scribes also had to learn what specific system of weights and measurements was in effect at the time. Kings would often standardize weights and measurements to their own liking when they came to the throne. Even if a standard system of weights and measures was in effect during a particular period, a scribe would have to know what weights and measures were in use in other cultures—in Elam, for example or, from Syria. Thus, traders would also have to know how to keep good, clear accounts of the goods that they traded and scribes would record what's coming in or out of the area that they were working in.

In addition to simple accounting, tablets record multiplication tables, division, reciprocals, and extracting square roots. More complex problems usually involved algebra rather than geometry, and we have a number of word problems, as well. These problems focused on specific cases, issues that had to be worked out, and they were not as interested in establishing a general formulation or a proof for a mathematical concept. For example, a common mathematical problem would be figuring out how much dirt had to be moved when a canal was enlarged or a new canal was constructed. Sometimes, the method of reckoning the answer is provided and, in those instances, we can understand that an experienced mathematician was writing out the word problem. More often, the number was provided, the solution was given, and in those instances, it seems as if a scribe was taking dictation or using a practice tablet in order to learn this particular sign. So, just like medicine, mathematics suffers from the fact that we don't have evidence all the time from practicing mathematicians, but instead scribes who needed to expand their knowledge so they could earn work in a palace.

With this interest in mathematics, it's a little surprising to learn that there wasn't a lot of focus on divining whether the answer was exactly right or approximate. I kind of like that about Babylonian math. If you're moving a lot of dirt, you move lots of dirt and a few extra shovelfuls here and there don't make much difference. Other mathematical concepts, such as the properties of the triangle, circle, and rectangle, were known and recognized by mathematicians, but again there wasn't much interest in discovering the more complex properties of surface and volume of these figures. That ties into this idea of guesstimation; this answer is close enough.

Mesopotamian math used the sexagesimal system. The meaning of a number depends on its position relative to other numbers. For example, the number five means something much different if there's a zero after it, 50, or two zeros after it, 500. Babylonian math was the only ancient mathematical system that developed this type of sexagesimal system that we use today. Another aspect of Babylonian math was that it was based on units of 60. The basic fundamental number was 60 and you might expect that, considering on how the penalties in the law are focused on a mina or shekels, and there are 60 shekels in a mina. So, the standard weight was also based on units of 60. The concept of zero was not developed until the 8th century B.C. and this missing link caused a lot of problems for Babylonian mathematicians. Some tablets leave a little space where a zero would be. There was clearly a recognition that something was missing—no pun intended—but once the concept of zero was developed, mathematicians avoided using it in the final position. We're not exactly sure why, but that, too, would cause problems in determining an exact number. Most of our evidence for math comes from word problems, probably because the texts were used in scribal schools.

Another aspect of Mesopotamian science was astronomy. This is the field in which the most precise evidence was collected. Kings and priests were especially interested in this science because it would allow them to predict the future or interpret omens. This aspect of astronomy connects the science directly with the practice of divination. Divination was one of the most important scientific disciplines developed in Mesopotamia and the one that would have been the most valuable because it would help make sense of the world. We've seen already in medicine that there is an intertwining of magic and science, so it is not surprising that, in the field of astronomy, there would also be a similar connection between the two issues.

Divination was the way that the gods communicated the destiny of individuals. It required a belief that the natural world had the potential to reveal future events and a diviner had to master many different skills in order to interpret a specific sign that was present in the environment that surrounded him. I'll give a couple of examples.

Animal entrails, especially livers, could be studied and interpreted to help predict the future. This practice occurred in other ancient cultures, as well. The liver is the largest organ, so it would seem to be the most important and have the most potential for revealing future events. Diviners also had to master different techniques, such as what it meant when oil was poured over water and how that oil spread in a specific pattern could give some insight into what you should do the next week or the next day. Diviners also looked at how smoke rose from incense, so it's this same idea of exploring a pattern, and that would reveal a meaning that could help you solve whatever question you were consulting the diviner about.

Numerous observations of animal behavior, such as how animals behaved when they approached the gates of a city or altar of a temple—and you can imagine if an animal was going to an altar of a temple, it was not going to be a happy outcome. They might be a little agitated and that was always seen as a bad sign because an animal should go willing to sacrifice. These behaviors of animals were observed, as were any reports of animals that had unusual markings. The birth of a cow with a specific marking would be reported to official diviners because this could portend the future, as well. Specific purification rituals could weaken or even prevent a bad outcome from an omen that was discovered. By looking at omens, diviners could try and change the future. This is an important element of divination that isn't emphasized enough, I think, because it seems as if all of these lists of omens and their meanings are always bad. Yet, the idea was to look at the future and try and stave off the bad event and instead replace it with a much more positive event.

We are best informed about divination through celestial observations. The Babylonian Astronomical Diaries are records of observations that astronomers in Babylon undertook from the Esagila, the temple of Marduk. These diviners would monitor and note any events that occurred either night or day in the sky. They would also note other environmental observations. Changes in the weather or the depth of the river would be noted down in these diaries as well. Many of these diaries are preserved from the 7th century on, although they're often in fragments. The Persians, who succeeded the Babylonians, picked up this interest in astronomy and expanded it. It was the Persians who came into contact with the

Greeks that really revealed Babylonian astronomy to the western Mediterranean.

The Babylonians, through this observation of the sky, created a lunar calendar. But, it was a lunar calendar that was based on a 19-year interval. So, for 12 years, there would be 12-month years; then, for 7 years, there would be 13-month years. It would create a 19-year calendar that was made up of 235 months. This would help resolve the issues with the lunar calendar and the intercalary months that are needed when one follows the moon instead of a solar calendar. Some of the observations that survive are focused on the appearance of a new moon. All of these observations have as the first part of the formula, "When the Moon appears on the first day, there will be silence, the land will be satisfied." But, the second part has many variants. Some of these are: "…when the day is long according to its calculation, there will be a long reign…" Or, "…when the Moon is relatively full, the crops of the land will prosper, the king will go to preeminence." Or, "…there will be an overthrowing of fortresses and the downfall of garrisons; there will be obedience and good-will in the land." Other lunar observations state that, "When a halo surrounds the Moon and Scorpio stands in it, it will cause men to marry princesses," or "lions will die, and the traffic of the land will be hindered." You can see there is quite a bit of wiggle room for these diviners and their predictions of the future; you can marry a princess or a lion will die somewhere.

Natural phenomena were especially troubling. "When the earth quakes…the king's land will revolt from him." Or, "When the earth quakes during the night, harm will come to the land, or devastation to the land." Long lists of these descriptions and interpretations exist to help future diviners understand the meaning of what they see. This really provides a background for the field of divination that we don't have for medicine or even mathematics. It also provides a sort of history; we can't always correlate a specific observation with a specific king, but we see that there's a strong interest in the past and what events were most momentous and how those events might reoccur in the future.

One of the most valuable achievements in astronomy could have been the ability to predict eclipses. The records of these eclipses are what we use to help establish a chronology for Mesopotamian history based on the date of the eclipse. Modern astronomers have been able to connect certain dates recorded in the Babylonian diaries and other astronomical texts with known eclipses. Unfortunately, there are three possible years for most of these events, so we remain uncertain about the exact year in which a specific event occurred. This is one of the reasons why we have three different chronologies. I mentioned this in an earlier lecture that there's a high chronology, a middle chronology, and a low chronology, and the framework for those chronologies is based on the different dates for the eclipses.

Much of the evidence for Mesopotamian scientific thought and literature was found in the library of the 7th-century B.C. Assyrian ruler, Assurbanipal, at Nineveh. Over 25,000 tablets were found in the palace of Assurbanipal and about half of these tablets were scientific or literary compositions. They form the bulk of the evidence from which we derive our knowledge of medicine, astronomy, and mathematics. Most of the texts that I've discussed today come from Assurbanipal's library. Several letters from Assurbanipal note his interest in collecting tablets. He told an official that he should seek out certain men in the city and they should, "seek out all the tablets, those in their houses and all those that are deposited in the temple…hunt for the valuable tablets…which do not exist in Assyria and send them to me…no one shall withhold a tablet from you." If you think of all of the records in temples that we've discussed in this course and all of those long ration lists, I'm sure that Assurbanipal got a lot of irrelevant information in the shipments of tablets that were sent to him. What he would have considered valuable would have been the scientific records and also literary compositions.

The collection from Nineveh is the largest single collection of tablets from Mesopotamia. It preserved the most complete versions of the Gilgamesh epic, for example, that we discussed right at the beginning of the course. A colophon—which is a heading that often gives the first line of a poem, or a letter, or some way of identifying the text—was added to many of the manuscripts that scribes copied for this library in Nineveh. Not only would Assurbanipal demand that his officials send him texts, but he had his scribes rewrite them. Some of these noted that the texts had been collected by Assurbanipal, but others were lengthier. One long colophon is addressed to the Assyrian god Nabu and states: "I, Assurbanipal, king of the universe, king of Assyria on whom [the gods] have bestowed vast intelligence, who acquired penetrating acumen for the most recondite details of scholarly erudition, no predecessors of whom among having any comprehension of such matters…I placed [the tablets] for the future in the library…for the well-being of my soul, to avoid disease, and to sustain the foundations of my royal house…when this work is deposited in your," in Nabu's, "house…look upon it and remember me with favor!" This colophon explicitly sets out that Assurbanipal wanted to use the information in the tablets for his own health—so that's why he would be interested in the medical texts—and his prosperity—presumably the omen lists would be especially useful for this. Assurbanipal is also interested in giving this information, this evidence, to future rulers. Just as Hammurabi is trying to create a legacy in which he's remembered for justice, Assurbanipal is focused on scientific thought and what he can give to future kings that they can use as a reference to help them rule better. It's a very interesting shift and seems to be specific to Assurbanipal. I'm sure you've also noted that he is very proud of his intelligence and like the Ur III ruler, Shulgi, Assurbanipal was one of the few literate kings. That's something to look forward to, as we move towards the Assyrian Empire.

In the next lecture, we will examine the literature that, together with science, was essential to the knowledge that Assurbanipal and other rulers collected. We've discussed certain types of literature, specifically royal inscriptions, law codes, also inscriptions that record military events, and even diplomatic letters. I think you've gotten a sense of some of the literature that has been preserved, but we will take a look at many other types of literature that give us more insight into daily life or poems that would have been especially favored by the Mesopotamians. They might explain the creation of the world or they might tell humorous stories. All of this gives us a sense of the richness of Sumerian literature that has survived.

Lecture Twenty-Four
Poetry and Literature

Scope:

As we will see in this lecture, the poetry and literature of Mesopotamia touched on a wide range of topics. We will investigate literature that explores such themes as creation and the deeds and personalities of the gods. Other poems examine the ideas of suffering, divine justice, or the effects of misrule by a king who has lost the favor of the gods. Proverbial wisdom, jokes, and love poems give insight into the concerns of daily life. Finally, magic spells were cast to ease the pain of a headache or to dismiss an annoying lawsuit. As we begin our study of Mesopotamian literature, keep in mind that even though many tablets are preserved, they are often broken, leaving us with line breaks or gaps in the narratives. Further, the language of Mesopotamian literature is often repetitive, but working one's way through the literature can be quite rewarding.

Outline

I. Several creation myths survive that credit different deities with the act of forming the world.

   A. The *Enuma Elish* is one of the most famous Mesopotamian creation myths. It was probably composed in the 2nd millennium B.C., around the time of Hammurabi, but the earliest surviving texts date to about 1200 B.C.

   B. The Babylonian deity Marduk plays a prominent role in this version of the creation story, although an Assyrian version replaces him with the national deity of the Assyrians, Ashur.

   C. The poem describes the mingling of the deities of freshwater, Apsu, and saltwater, Tiamat, to create the first gods and form the horizon of the Earth.

   D. As more gods were formed, they began to annoy Apsu and Tiamat, who decided to kill them; instead, Apsu was killed, and the freshwater associated with him became the foundations of the first temple.

   E. Marduk is born from this first generation of gods and will become their champion to protect them from the angry

Tiamat. In return, he will become the leader, or king, of the gods. This creation myth both explains the formation of the world and justifies the office of kingship, locating it specifically in Babylon.

F. Marduk slays Tiamat and splits her body to form the sky and to run beneath the Earth. Afterward, he arranges the sun, moon, and stars in the sky, then creates humans to serve the gods. Finally, he decrees that 300 gods will live in the heavens and 300 will live on Earth with humans.

G. The gods reward Marduk's hard work with a temple in Babylon and a feast.

II. Several stories revolve around the idea of a struggle for, or loss of, kingship among the gods. These must have been useful ways of explaining the political chaos that sometimes occurred in Mesopotamia.

A. "Anzu, the Bird Who Stole Destiny" describes how Enlil temporarily lost the tablet that controlled destiny, a symbol of Enlil's kingship, when it was taken by the bird Anzu.

B. Anzu was an extremely ugly, eagle-like bird who had been created during the Great Flood. Enlil brought him to guard his palace; Anzu watched as Enlil assigned different duties to the gods, while he himself held the tablet of destiny.

C. Anzu stole the tablet while Enlil was in his bath and flew off with it. The poem reports, "Enlil was speechless," and the gods were dejected in the resulting chaos, but they refused to face Anzu and retrieve the tablet. The poem notes the increasing depression of the gods, giving us some sense of what can happen during a hiatus between rulers.

D. The warrior god Ninurta finally agreed to meet Anzu, and eventually the tablet was restored to Enlil.

E. In these stories of the gods, we see representations in the heavens of some of the same difficulties experienced on Earth.

III. One especially moving type of literature is the lament for a city when it has suffered destruction or invasion. The suffering of individuals is also recounted in several poems.

A. Such laments often describe the complete destruction of cities and the devastation of the population, but the archaeological record does not bear out this level of damage.

B. It is customary to frame these laments in terms of the abandonment of the city by its patron deity.

C. The poems of individual suffering often show a resigned acceptance that human pain, sickness, and poverty are inescapable if decreed by the gods. A Babylonian dialogue between a suffering man and a friend presents the difficult question of why the gods punish the righteous.

    1. The sufferer wallows in poverty and sees the wealthy ignoring the gods but prospering.

    2. His friend suggests that humans cannot understand the intentions of the gods and that it is possible for the gods to change an individual's fortune even within the course of a year. The sufferer accepts this philosophy, vows to be pious, and prays for relief.

D. These poems illustrate the universal difficulties of life and the eternal question of why the good and faithful must suffer, although the answer usually involves accepting that one cannot know the will of the gods.

IV. Other genres of literature, such as humorous stories, jokes, love poems, and magic spells, take a lighter view of life.

A. For example, an older scribe describes himself to a younger one as an ideal student, but we can imagine that the speaker might not have been as attentive as he asserts.

B. Another common genre of literature takes the form of debates between improbable creatures or concepts. In one dialogue between Summer and Winter, the two seasons argue over whose work is harder.

C. Humor can be one of the more difficult cultural elements to recover, but in Mesopotamia, we can see examples of social satire, as well as more obvious jokes.

    1. The interaction between different economic classes was fodder for many stories, such as the visit of a wealthy man who gives detailed instructions to his cleaners.

    2. His instructions are so explicit and lengthy that the cleaner is offended and suggests that the man do the cleaning himself.

D. Drinking songs were also a source of humor; one song waxes enthusiastic about the joy of drinking beer.

E. Finally, we see humor in Mesopotamian proverbs.

    1. On authority: "Whatever the man in authority said, it was not pleasant."

    2. On changes in profession: "A disgraced scribe becomes an incantation priest. A disgraced singer becomes a flute-player. A disgraced merchant becomes a con-man."

    3. On health: "To be sick is all right, to be pregnant is painful, to be pregnant and sick is just too much."

F. Love poetry can be set in a beautiful garden, beneath cedar trees, with nature creating a romantic mood.

    1. A poem about the wedding between Nabu, son of Marduk, and Tashmetu describes a garden with cedar, cypress, and juniper trees.

    2. Tashmetu wears gold earrings and bracelets of carnelian, prompting Nabu to ask, "Why are you so adorned, my Tashmetu? She replies, "So I can go to the garden with you, my Nabu…and there bind fast, hitch up, bind your days to the garden…bind your nights to the exquisite garden."

V. Magic spells were used to help ease the annoyances of life.

A. Spells to cure a headache, fever, or other illnesses are frequent and tell us about some of the maladies from which Mesopotamians suffered.

    1. "Cloudy eyes, blurred eyes, bloodshot eyes! Why do you cloud over? Why do you blur? Why do sand of river, pollen of date palm, pollen of fig tree, straw of winnower sting you?"

    2. "Headache, applied in heaven, removed in the netherworld, which sapped the strength of the strong young man, which has not returned her energy to the beautiful young woman…who will remove it, who will cast it out?"

B. In a spell by an *ashipu*, we learn that he was called in to remove the moral flaw that caused sickness.

C. Other spells drove away evil spirits and ghosts.

VI. This lecture has given us a taste of the different types of literature preserved from Mesopotamia.

    A. In this body of literature, we find many more myths and stories of the gods than any other form of non-royal literature. In them are also descriptions of the landscape, reminding us of the extraordinary natural setting of Mesopotamia.

    B. Even though the environment was abundant, other stories and poems relate extreme poverty and misery, whether from illness or unrequited love. The gods were more often a source of pain than relief, as the poem of the righteous sufferer conveys.

    C. This survey of literature gives us a glimpse of the philosophy or outlook on life in Mesopotamia, which can seem very negative. Some forms of literature, however, mitigate this pessimism with humor and an appreciation for natural beauty.

Essential Reading:

Benjamin Foster, *From Distant Days: Myths, Tales and Poetry of Ancient Mesopotamia.*

Graham Cunningham, et al., *The Literature of Ancient Sumer.*

Supplementary Reading:

Piotr Michalowski, "Sumerian Literature: An Overview," in *CANE*, vol. IV, pp. 2279–2292.

Jean Bottéro, "Akkadian Literature: An Overview," in *CANE*, vol. IV, pp. 2293–2304.

Questions to Consider:

1. How does this literature expand our understanding of the role of the gods in Mesopotamian life and thought?

2. What genres of literature represent the concerns of ordinary life, and what issues are described in them?

Lecture Twenty-Four—Transcript
Poetry and Literature

Our attention so far in this course has been focused on royal inscriptions, laws, bureaucratic records, and some letters between individuals. I hope that this gives you a taste of what the kings were interested in, but of course, they were just one group that wrote literature that has survived. In this lecture, we will consider the other types of literature that we know from Mesopotamia.

Remember that even though tablets are preserved because they are made from clay, they do break; so, if you pick up a translation of Mesopotamian poetry or other types of literature, you'll see that there are breaks in the line or large gaps that are missing. This can make Mesopotamian literature seem even more difficult, even more remote from something that we can understand. Still, I would encourage you to keep working through the poetry and to continue with that because it is a reward at the end. You get a much better sense of the Mesopotamian sense of poetry, the beauty and the culture that survives in this literature. Another challenge to the modern reader is that the language is quite repetitive and, as I'm sure you've guessed already, the names are a little difficult to pronounce; but, again, keep going through it because it's worth it.

In this lecture, we will begin with myths, creation myths, and other stories of the gods. This is probably the largest corpus of Sumerian literature because the Sumerians, Babylonians, and their successors were interested in what the gods did to provide a model for their own actions on earth. Several creation myths survive that credit different deities with the act of forming the world. The *Enuma Elish* is one of the most famous Mesopotamian creation myths. It was probably composed during the 2nd millennium B.C., maybe around the time of Hammurabi. Yet, the earliest surviving texts date to about 1200 B.C., so significantly later than the story is supposed to present. The Babylonian deity Marduk plays a prominent role in this version of the creation story, although an Assyrian version will replace him with their national deity, Ashur. Again, the connection between religion and politics can be seen even in this literature focused on explaining the creation of the world.

The poem describes the mingling of two types of water: the Apsu, which is fresh water, and Tiamat, the goddess of salt water. These two gods created the first deities and they also formed the horizon of the earth. So, if you look out on the sea, you can see that it is sky and water, so it's not surprising that these water deities would be prominent in the creation. As the gods were formed from these two water deities, they began to annoy Apsu and Tiamat and they decided to kill them. This is very much like the flood story that we discussed a while ago in which Enlil created humans to do work for them, but then they were noisy so he decided to get rid of them. Instead, Apsu was killed and the fresh water that he represented became the foundations of the first temple. So, right from the beginning of creation, we see the connection with the gods and also with temples and cities.

Marduk is born from this first generation of gods and he will become their champion to protect them from the angry Tiamat—who, of course, is quite annoyed that Apsu has been killed. In return for taking on this challenge, Marduk will become the leader or the king of the gods. So, this creation myth explains both the formation of the world and also justifies the office of kingship, locating it specifically in Babylon. This contrasts with the Early Dynastic focus on Enlil at Nippur. Marduk slays Tiamat; he splits her body to form the sky and to run beneath the earth. Afterwards, Marduk arranges the sun, the moon, and the stars in the sky, and he creates humans to serve the gods. Finally, Marduk decrees that 300 gods will live in the heavens and 300 gods will live on earth with humans. The gods reward Marduk's hard work—he's done quite a bit, setting the stars in the sky and also arranging who's going to live where—and so, as a reward for this, they sponsor a feast in his temple at Babylon.

Several stories revolve around the idea of the struggle for or loss of kingship among the gods. These must have been very useful ways to try and explain or understand the political chaos that could occur in Mesopotamia. Anzu, "The Bird Who Stole Destiny," describes how Enlil temporarily lost the tablet that controlled destiny. This tablet was a symbol of Enlil's kingship. Anzu was an extremely ugly eagle-like bird, who had been created during the Great Flood. He's sort of like a Mesopotamian concept of a dinosaur or a dragon, but there's a lot of emphasis on how ugly he is. Enlil brought him to the palace to guard it. Anzu stood at the door and would watch as Enlil assign different duties to the gods, while Enlil held the tablet of destiny. The poem records:

Enlil entrusted him with the entrance…he was wont to bath in pure waters before him. [This is Enlil taking a bath in front of Anzu.] Anzu's eyes looked upon the trappings of supremacy…on the tablet of destinies he was wont to gaze…He resolved in his heart to make off with supremacy! 'I myself will take the gods' tablet of destinies, I will gather to myself the responsibilities of all of the gods, I will have the throne for myself and take power over authority'.

Anzu stole the tablet of destiny while Enlil was in his bath and flew off with it. "Enlil was speechless," the poem notes. The other gods were quite dejected in the chaos that resulted from this, but they refused to face Anzu and retrieve the tablet themselves. So, we're in a position where no one is taking charge. No one is willing to tackle Anzu and try and restore the tablet of destinies to its rightful owner. The poem notes the increasing depression of the gods and this can give us a sense of what might have happened in a hiatus between rulers—say, during an uncertain succession from father to son when no one is in charge. The warrior god Ninurta finally agreed to meet Anzu. Ninurta faced a very difficult challenge, since the tablet allowed Anzu to change the direction of any arrows that Ninurta used against him. Anzu would simply order the arrows, "shaft which has come, go back to your thicket…because he was holding the tablet of destinies…battle died down, attack died down." If Anzu is controlling the future, then he should be able to very effectively prevent anyone from attacking him and killing him. This caused a consultation and the god Ea suggested to Ninurta that he cut off Anzu's wings, so that when Anzu ordered the feathers to come to reattach themselves, the arrows that also had feathers on their shaft would be included in the command and that would kill Anzu. This is exactly what Ninurta decided to do and the tablet was restored to Enlil.

We see in the stories of the gods that there's a lot of interest in representing in the heavens some of the difficulties—especially, the problems concerning kingship—that happened on earth in the society of the gods. Since the gods are associated so closely with cities, one especially moving type of literature is the lament for a city when it has suffered destruction or invasion. The suffering of individuals is also recorded in several poems. The poems that describe a lament for a city often go into great detail about how a city is completely removed or its walls are taken down. You get the impression from the lament that the entire population has been killed and the city taken down. As I said, this makes for a very moving poem, but it is almost always an exaggeration; we don't find very often any archaeological correspondence for this level of destruction. But, the interest in describing the details of the distress of the occupants shows how devastating it could be when an enemy did attack a city.

It is customary to frame the lament in terms of the abandonment of the city by its patron deity. You might recall that we talked about this very early on in the course. If a city is associated specifically with a god or a goddess and it suffers some destruction or threat, then that would seem to indicate that the god or goddess could not really protect the city very effectively. And so, the idea occurred that a city could only be attacked or fall when its patron deity abandoned it. The details of the destruction inflicted on cities are provided. Temples are defaced and robbed of their cult statues, city gates are destroyed, and the city itself can be described as being burned or even flooded with its own irrigation canals. So, once again, we see the importance of the irrigation canals; they can be turned as a weapon against its own inhabitants.

A lament for the city of Ur describes the catastrophe that occurred at the end of the Ur III dynasty, when "the city was made into ruins…its people, not potsherd, filled its sides…in all its streets, where they used to promenade, dead bodies were lying about; in the palaces where the festivities of the land took place, the people lay in heaps. In the city, the wife was abandoned, the son was abandoned, the possessions were scattered about." In this lament, the patron deity of Ur sees the damage and weeps for the city, but she was unable to prevent its destruction because it had been destined by the gods. This is the only way that a patron deity would leave a city, if the gods had decreed that the city must be destroyed, often because the ruler was impious or simply because it was time for the kingship in that city to end.

Moving from the suffering of a city to the suffering of an individual, we have a number of poems that show how Mesopotamian citizens tried to deal with the problems of human pain, sickness, and poverty. These inflictions are inescapable if they are decreed by the gods, just as the destruction of a city cannot be prevented. A Babylonian dialogue between a suffering man and a friend presents the difficult question of why the gods punish the righteous. The sufferer wallows in poverty. He tells his friend:

> My energies have turned feeble, my prosperity is at a standstill…beer, the sustenance of mankind, is far from being enough…have I withheld my offerings? I prayed to my god." The poor man sees the wealthy man ignoring the gods, but prospering. He says, "Those who seek not after a god can go the road of favor…a fool is ahead of me, rogues are in the ascendant, I am demoted.

The friend suggests that humans cannot understand the intentions of the gods and that it is possible for the gods to change fortune even within the course of a year. He tells his suffering friend, "…Your logic is perverse, you have cast off justice, you have scorned divine design. In your emotional state you have an urge to disregard divine ordinances…the strategy of a god is as remote as innermost heaven, the command of a goddess cannot be drawn out." After a great deal of back and forth, the sufferer accepts this philosophy; he vows to continue being pious and to pray for some relief from his current condition. These poems illustrate the universal difficulties of life and questioning of why the good and faithful must suffer. The answer usually involves accepting that it is impossible to know the will of the gods and some invocation or prayer for hope for future change.

Other genres of literature—humorous stories, jokes, love poems, and magic spells—take a lighter view of life. Scribes often write about their lives and these are preserved in the tablets of scribal schools most often. One young student is explaining how he behaves as a student. He says to a current student he's teaching:

> Like you, I was once a youth and had a mentor. The teacher assigned a task to me—it was man's work. Like a springing reed, I leapt up and put myself to work. I did not depart from my teacher's instructions, and I did not start doing things on my own initiative…I did whatever he outlined for me—everything was always in its place. Only a fool would have deviated from his instructions.

Clearly, this is an idealized version of what students actually undertook. We know from the many mistakes and even comments about teachers that survive on tablets from scribal school that not every student was quite as attentive.

Another common genre of literature is a debate between either improbable creatures or concepts. In this dialogue between Summer and Winter, the two seasons—who are, of course, personified, as all nature was—argue over whose work was harder. Winter was feeling especially put upon and he says that he was overcome by anger and he started a quarrel with Summer.

> Summer, my brother, you should not praise yourself…you should not brag. As if you were the one who had done the hard work, as if you had done the farming, as if you had taken care of irrigation control during the spring floods, as if you had brought forth the…grain in the arable tracts with the dew from heaven—how much through my toil is it that you enter the palace!

Clearly, Winter is feeling a little unappreciated and Summer taunts Winter by claiming that he's not only the better season because he produces the harvest, but he's the more popular season because people stay out later. They want his arrival and, during winter, they huddle in their houses and sleep all of the time. Winter gets increasingly angry and, finally, Enlil intervenes to settle the dispute and they enjoy a banquet. The poem concludes: "Enlil answered Summer and Winter," saying "'Winter is controller of the life-giving waters of all the lands—the farmer of the gods produces everything. Summer, my son, how can you compare yourself to your brother Winter?'…Summer bowed to Winter and offered him a prayer. In his house he prepared emmer-beer and wine." You can imagine that with the focus on agriculture in Mesopotamia, this would be a dialogue that farmers might engage in, saying which season was the most profitable for them. Could they produce their harvest without all of the seasons? These dialogues give some insight into sort of matters of philosophical debate in Mesopotamia.

Humor is one of the most difficult cultural concepts to recover, but in Mesopotamia, we get examples of social satire, as well as more obvious jokes. The obvious jokes are focused on bodily humor—flatulence, the sort of universal concepts that make teenagers giggle. The interaction between different economic classes was fodder for many stories, such as the visit of a wealthy man to his cleaners. The man gives detailed instructions describing the steps involved in washing his clothes. The wealthy man says:

You should lay flat the fringe and the border...you should soak the thin part in a brew, you should strain that with a strainer...you should split the seam and cool it, you should dry it in the cool of the evening, lest the weaving get too stiffened by the sun.

He's clearly going beyond the usual light or heavy starch question that we might engage in our cleaners with. The wealthy man's instructions are so explicit and lengthy that the cleaner is offended and suggests that the man do the cleaning himself. "What you ordered me to do I could not narrate, declaim, speak or repeat...come now...let me show you a place [where] the big job you have on your hands you can set to yourself." These interactions between wealthy and poor men usually result in the embarrassment of the wealthy man at the hands of the poor man.

Another type of literature for which we have a few examples is drinking songs, and we've discussed how important beer was in Mesopotamian culture. One drinking song waxes enthusiastic about the effects and the joy of drinking beer. "We will have the cupbearers, the boys and the brewers stand by. As I spin around the lake of beer, while feeling wonderful, feeling wonderful, while drinking beer, in a blissful mood, while drinking alcohol and feeling exhilarated, with joy in the heart and a contented liver—my heart is a heart filled with joy! I clothe my contented liver in a garment fit for a queen!" It's hard to top that as a drinking song that explains the feeling of the effects of beer.

Other types of literature can be either humorous or try to dispense advice, and many proverbs are preserved from Mesopotamia. One proverb begins, "Whatever the man in authority said, it was not pleasant." Here we get a contrast to all of those laws that are set out by kings establishing order. Clearly, common wisdom was that whoever was in authority was going to say something that wasn't to your benefit. On changes in professions, a proverb indicates, "A disgraced scribe becomes an incantation priest. A disgraced singer becomes a flute-player. A disgraced merchant becomes a con-man." So, all of the accounting and interactions that we've seen with merchants can result in deception. Some proverbs are focused on health. "To be sick is all right, to be pregnant is painful; to be pregnant and sick is just too much." Clearly, morning sickness was an issue that was seen to be something that was too hard to endure.

Love poetry can be set in a beautiful garden beneath cedar trees and anything that creates a romantic mood for the man and woman involved. A wedding between Nabu—the son of Marduk and the patron deity of scribes—and his wife Tashmetu describes a garden that contained the shade of cedar and cypress and juniper trees. Tashmetu wears gold earrings and bracelets of carnelian. Nabu asks, "Why are you so adorned my Tashmetu? So I can go to the garden with you my Nabu...and there bind fast, hitch up, bind your days to the garden...bind your nights to the exquisite garden." This sense of nature pervades love poetry and also some of the other stories that we have seen already. It creates a much more vivid sense of the environment that the Mesopotamians enjoyed.

Finally, magic spells were used to help ease the annoyances of life. Spells to cure a headache, fever, or other illnesses are frequent, and they tell us about some of the maladies that were most common. For all you allergy sufferers out there: "Cloudy eyes, blurred eyes, bloodshot eyes! Why do you cloud over, why do you blur? Why do sand of river, pollen of date palm, pollen of fig tree, straw of winnower sting you." There's a lot of discussion about eye problems. Another common affliction was a headache. "Headache, applied in heaven, removed in the netherworld, which sapped the strength of the strong young man, which has not returned her energy to the beautiful young woman...who will remove it, who will cast it out?" These spells also report some of the incantations that the ashipu—remember that is the magician or the priest who would come to consult anyone who was sick—these are some of the incantations that he might say over an ill person. "I have lit a fire, I have set up a brazier, I have burned the absolving minerals...just as I damped the brazier I lit, just as I put out the fire I kindled...may the disease, the curse...be released and absolution be brought about." Other spells would drive away generic evil; some even got rid of ghosts that were rattling around the houses. One spell was designed to prevent an opponent in a lawsuit from speaking. "...My adversary, until I slap his cheek, until I rip out his tongue, until I send his words back into his mouth, I will not allow his mouth to speak." You can imagine someone muttering this on the way into the law courts or the assembly, wherever the case was being adjudicated, and trying to get the upper hand on his opponent.

In this lecture, we've seen many different types of literature are preserved. Most of the literature that survives concerns myths and stories of the gods and this, next to royal literature, forms the bulk of stories that survive from Mesopotamia. In them, there are many descriptions of the landscape and this reminds us of what an extraordinary natural setting it was. Even though the environment was abundant, however, other stories and poems relate extreme poverty and misery either from illness; sometimes from unrequited love—most often on the side of the female rather than the male. The gods were more often a source of pain than relief, but there was still great interest in how they lived and what sort of society they created. Spells attempted to ward off evils and humor could temporarily ease the situation. Some of this literature also gives us an idea of the philosophy that was present in Mesopotamia. Sometimes, Mesopotamian cultures can seem very pessimistic. If you get ill, you're going to die. If the moon rises in a certain quarter, your kingdom will be destroyed. There are a lot of negative outcomes that are recorded in texts that are most commonly presented in surveys. I think if we consider the other types of literature, we get a much richer sense of what the philosophy was like. That, sure, there were pessimistic moments and there was a lot of pain and suffering, but there was also humor to be found in situations, there was beauty in nature, and there was also love that would bind a family together.

In our next lecture, we're going to focus on literature of a different sort, and we're going to jump ahead about 400 years from the reign of Hammurabi. The intervening period was somewhat of a dark age—we'll explore that in more detail. The letters that survive from the 14th century focus on the correspondence of rulers. We will see that the rulers of Babylonia have close diplomatic contacts with the kings of Egypt and other kings in the Near East that help them negotiate their standing with each other.

Maps

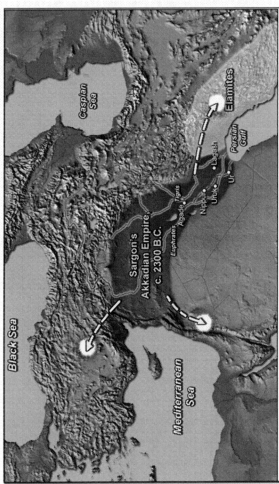

Sargon of Akkad

Sargon of Akkad (r. c. 2334-2279) enjoyed an unusually long reign, during which he conquered a vast territory encompassing most of the Fertile Crescent. Whether this can be properly termed an empire depends on how *empire* is defined. Sargon may not have intended to impose a coherent system of governance on deliberately conquered territory as the term suggests. But Akkadian campaigns into Anatolia, Elam, and the Levant continued during his reign and those of his successors. Sargon established his own capital at Agade (Akkad), which has not yet been located, although it is believed to be near or beneath Baghdad.

Akkadian Expansion under Naram-Sin

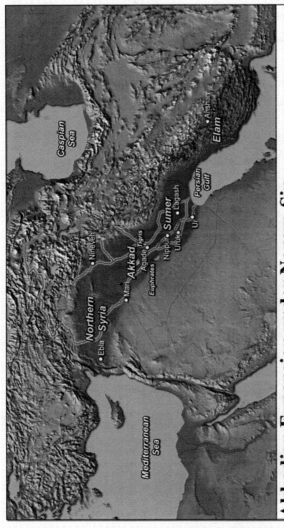

Naram-Sin (r. c. 2254-2218 B.C.), Sargon's grandson, dubbed himself "King of the Four Quarters of the World," and during his reign, he indeed ruled over Elam, Sumer, Akkad, and parts of Northern Syria. His focus was on securing trade routes; control of Elam ensured access to the Indus Valley in India, while key trading cities like Mari and Ebla were hubs of Syrian commerce. He successfully suppressed revolts in the city-states of Sumer and proved a quite capable ruler. It was his representation of himself as divine, on inscriptions and in visual media, that probably explains later hostile accounts that blame him for the collapse of Akkadian power, which occurred around 2190 B.C.

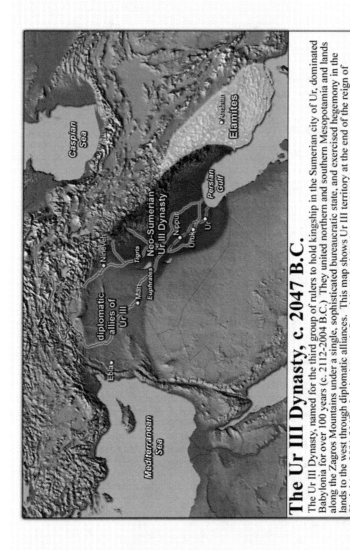

The Ur III Dynasty, c. 2047 B.C.

The Ur III Dynasty, named for the third group of rulers to hold kingship in the Sumerian city of Ur, dominated Babylonia for over 100 years (c. 2112-2004 B.C.) They united northern and southern Mesopotamia and lands along the Zagros Mountains under a single, sophisticated bureaucratic state, and exercised hegemony in the lands to the west through diplomatic alliances. This map shows Ur III territory at the end of the reign of Shulgi (r. c. 2094-2047), the single most influential ruler of the dynasty. Shulgi presided over innovations in taxation, territorial expansion, provincial administration, and record-keeping. The Ur III dynasty eventually fell due to outside pressures on its borders, especially from Elam, and internal economic disruption.

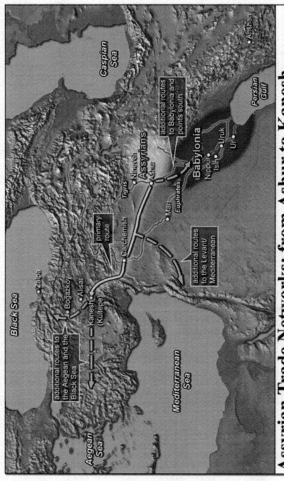

Assyrian Trade Networks: from Ashur to Kanesh

Long before the heyday of the great Assyrian Empire of the 1st millennium B.C., during the Old Assyrian Period (20th–19th centuries B.C.), private merchant activity flourished along a primary trade route between the Assyrian city of Ashur and the trade outpost of Kanesh in Anatolia. Donkey caravans loaded with tin, gold, silver, and Assyrian-made textiles traversed mountain passes to arrive at a merchant *karum* at Kanesh. The karum was a kind of lower city, separate from the area occupied by the Anatolian rulers. This primary Ashur-Kanesh route was supplemented by additional routes north and west from Kanesh, south from Ashur into Babylonia, and by additional routes into Levantine regions.

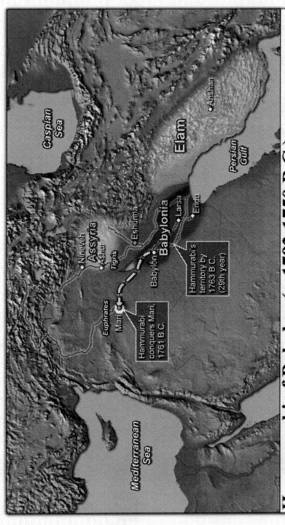

Hammurabi of Babylon (r. 1792–1750 B.C.)

When Hammurabi took the throne, he inherited a city-state controlling little more than the city of Babylon and the surrounding area. By 1765, he had led a coalition against Elam, which had been a threatening neighbor for some time. In 1763, aided by Zimri-Lim of Mari, he ended Rim-Sin's reign in Larsa. This made Babylonia a regional power controlling most of southern Mesopotamia. In 1761, Hammurabi turned on his former ally Zimri-Lim, conquering Mari, expanding Babylonian hegemony further north and securing the riverine trade routes upon which Babylonian prosperity depended. The state Hammurabi founded would endure for another century and a half.

Labels on the map: Caspian Sea; Elam; Anshan; Persian Gulf; Assyria; Nineveh; Ashur; Tigris; Eshnunna; Babylonia; Babylon; Larsa; Eridu; Hammurabi's territory by 1763 B.C. (29th year); Euphrates; Mari; Hammurabi conquers Mari, 1761 B.C.; Mediterranean Sea

Timeline

c. 9000 B.C. ....Neolithic period begins

c. 6000–5400................................Halaf period

c. 6000–4000................................Ubaid period

c. 3500–3000................................Uruk period

c. 2900–2350................................Early Dynastic period

c. 2500...Royal Cemetery at Ur

r. c. 2450–2425 ....Eannatum

c. 2334–2190................................Akkadian/Sargonic period

r. c. 2334–2279 ....Sargon of Akkad

r. c. 2254–2218 ....Naram-Sin

r. c. 2100 ....Gudea of Lagash

c. 2112–2004................................Ur III

r. c. 2094–2047 ....Shulgi

c. 2004–1595................................Old Babylonian era

c. 1910–1740................................Karum Kanesh levels II and Ib

c. 1800–1762................................Mari archives

r. 1792–1750 ....Hammurabi

c. 1595–1375................................Dark Age

c. 1800–1155................................Kassite/Middle   Babylonian/Middle Assyrian

c. 1365–1335................................Amarna archive

c. 1200..."Sea Peoples"

c. 1155–626..................................Neo-Assyrian Empire

r. c. 721–705 ....Sargon II

625–539 ....Neo-Babylonian era

539–332 ....Persian Empire

333 ....Battle of Issus

331–143 ....Alexander and successors (Alexander became king of Persia in 331)

c. 312–63...................................Seleucids

c. 250 B.C.–A.D. 224.................Parthians

c. A.D. 224–651 ....Sassanians

c. A.D. 651–present ....Arabs

Note: The primary sources for dating are Michael Roaf, *Cultural Atlas of Mesopotamia and the Ancient Near East*, and Marc Van De Mieroop, *A History of the Ancient Near East, c. 3000–323 BC*. Professor Castor uses the middle chronology for the most part. Dating is inherently problematic for Mesopotamian history, however, and the majority of dates are approximate.

Glossary

Adad: Rain god.

Akkad: Region of northern Mesopotamia; rose to power under Sargon in the 23rd century B.C.

Akkadian: One of the two main languages used in Mesopotamian literature.

Amorite: Nomadic tribes from the western desert who occupied Babylonia in the 20th century B.C.

An/Anu: God of the sky.

Anatolia: Term for modern Turkey (together with Asia Minor); usually used for the inland regions of Turkey, especially above the Taurus Mountains.

Apsu/Abzu: God who personifies sweet water that runs beneath the Earth.

Aramaic: Semitic language that became widespread in the Near East during the 12th century B.C.; it used an alphabetic, rather than cuneiform, script.

Ashipu: A priest or diviner, consulted to determine the supernatural cause of an illness and to cast spells against it.

Ashur: Capital of the Assyrian Empire and the name of the national god of the Assyrians.

Asia Minor: Ancient name for the area of modern Turkey, especially the western coast.

Asu: A physician who treated the physical (as opposed to the supernatural) aspects of a malady.

Babylon: Capital city of Babylonia.

Babylonia: Region of southern and the lower part of northern Mesopotamia (the lands of the 3rd-millennium B.C. states of Sumer and Akkad).

Bala: System of tax and redistribution established in the Ur III period.

Behistun Decree: Trilingual inscription of Darius I in modern Iran that was the key to the decipherment of cuneiform by Henry Rawlinson. Sometimes spelled Besitun.

Bulla: Round, hollow clay lump that either contains tokens or is stamped with a number of tokens. Plural: *bullae*.

City-state: Political unit centered on one or, perhaps, more than one city and the surrounding territory. This was the dominant form of political control in the 3rd and early 2nd millennia B.C.

Corvée labor: The practice of gathering large numbers of workers for a specific project.

Cuneiform: A syllabic script used to write Sumerian, Akkadian, and Babylonian languages.

Cylinder seal: Engraved cylinder, often of semiprecious stone, that was rolled over clay as a mark of an authority.

Dagan: Akkadian god of grain.

Dumuzi: Spouse of Ishtar; Dumuzi is the god of vegetation and spends half of the year in the netherworld.

É: Temple, house of the god.

Edubba: A scribal school.

Elam: State that controlled southwestern Iran.

En/ensi: Sumerian word for governor or king.

Enki: Sumerian god of water; also of intelligence, science, and crafts.

Enkidu: Hero created by the gods who lived in the steppe until he came to Uruk and became the friend of Gilgamesh.

Enlil: Patron deity of Nippur, god of kingship, king of the gods and heavens.

Enuma Elish: Epic poem that described the creation of the world.

Gilgamesh: Hero of the first epic; ruler of Uruk, who had many adventures and attempted, unsuccessfully, to learn the secret of immortality.

Gutians: Nomadic tribe from the Zagros Mountains that was blamed for the end of the Akkadian Dynasty.

Hittites: Civilization centered in Anatolia and flourishing from about the 18th to the 12th centuries B.C.

Inanna/Ishtar: Goddess of carnal love and war; the patron goddess of Uruk.

Isin: City in southern Mesopotamia.

Karum: Akkadian word for a colony, trading post, or marketplace established by Old Assyrian era merchants.

Kassites: Nomadic tribespeople who moved into Babylonia after about the 18th century B.C. After the Hittites sacked Babylon in 1595 B.C., the Kassites slowly took control and ruled until the 12th century B.C.

Lagash: City in southern Mesopotamia.

Lapis lazuli: A semiprecious blue stone available only through trade with the eastern regions in modern Afghanistan; lapis was prized as a luxury object.

Larsa: City in southern Mesopotamia.

Law code: Collection of laws published by a king or gathered in an archive.

Lugal: Sumerian word for big man, used for kings.

Marduk: Patron deity of Babylon.

Mari: Ancient Mesopotamian city, located along the northern Euphrates River in modern Syria.

Medes: An Iranian group who helped to overthrow the Assyrians in the 7th century B.C. and ruled Mesopotamia with the Persians.

Merodoch-baladan II: King of Babylonia in the 8th century B.C. who rebelled against the Assyrian rulers Sargon and Sennacherib.

Misharum: A dispensation given by a king that allowed taxes to revert back to a previous rate. It was customary for a king to enact a *misharum* in his first year of rule.

Naditum: A priestess who spent her life in service to the temple of a god or goddess.

Nanna: Patron deity of Ur.

Nimrud: Assyrian capital that flourished in the reign of Ashurnasirpal II in the 9th century B.C.; home of Ashurnasirpal's library.

Nineveh: An Assyrian city with a large palace built by the 8th-century ruler Sennacherib.

Ningirsu: God of Lagash.

Ninkasi: Patron goddess of brewers.

Ninurta: Mesopotamian war god.

Nippur: Religious capital of Mesopotamia; home of the patron deity Enlil.

Persepolis: A Persian capital city in Iran founded by Darius I around 518 B.C. The best preserved of all the Persian capital cities.

Persians: An Iranian group who came to prominence in the 6th century B.C. under the leadership of Cyrus and governed all of the Near East until defeated by Alexander the Great in the 4th century B.C.

Proskynesis: Ritual prostration.

Protome: Head or forepart of a human or animal body.

Royal Cemetery: Group of large, lavish Early Dynastic burials of the ruling elite of the city of Ur, c. 2500 B.C.

Satrapy: Persian term for a province; these regions were governed by *satraps*.

Sealings: The strips of clay over which stamp seals were rolled to indicate that a sign of authority was needed.

Shagina: Military governor of a province during the Ur III period (2112–2004 B.C.)

Shamash: The sun god and god of justice; the patron deity of Sippar.

Shara: God of Umma.

Sin: The Sumerian moon god; this deity became especially prominent during the reign of Nabonidus in the 6th century B.C.

Stratigraphy: The study of different layers, or strata, that indicate a period of occupation. The strata closest to the surface are the most recent.

Sumer: Southern Mesopotamia and the homeland of the Sumerian language.

Sumerian: Together with Akkadian, the other major written language used in Mesopotamian literature.

Sumerian king list: List created in the 2nd millennium B.C. that describes mythical and historical rulers in Mesopotamia. The main purpose of the list is to show an uninterrupted transfer of power from one king to another.

Susa: Capital city of the Elamites of western Iran.

Temple-state theory: The now-outdated theory that only temples could own land.

Tiamat: A goddess who personifies saltwater; her body was split in two to create the Earth.

Tell: Mound of earth that marks the site of an abandoned ancient city.

Token: A small clay marker used to record quantities of a specific object.

Ubaid: Culture (4000–3500 B.C.) named after the pottery found at Tell al-Ubaid in southern Mesopotamia.

Ur: City in southern Mesopotamia, near the ancient mouth of the Tigris and Euphrates Rivers.

Uruk phenomenon: Describes the 4th-millennium development of urbanization in southern Mesopotamia centered at the city of Uruk.

Ziggurat: A form of temple that stands atop a stepped platform; ziggurats are likely the source of the biblical Tower of Babel.

Biographical Notes

Alexander the Great (b. 356–d. 323 B.C.): King of Macedonia (r. 336–323 B.C.) who invaded Asia Minor and defeated the last Persian king at the battle of Gaugamela in 331. Alexander took control of the Persian Empire and took his army further east to India. He died in Babylon in 323 B.C.

Ashurbanipal (r. c. 668–627 B.C.): Son of the Assyrian ruler Esarhaddon, Ashurbanipal was challenged by his brother, who allied with the Elamites and the Babylonians to rebel against him. The revolt was put down, and Ashurbanipal led a campaign against the capital of Elam, Susa. Official Assyrian records stop in 639 B.C., although Ashurbanipal ruled another 12 years.

Ashurnasirpal II (r. 883–859 B.C.): Assyrian ruler who founded a new capital at Nimrud, led annual campaigns, and focused much of his attention on controlling the west, especially Israel and Judah.

Cambyses: Persian ruler (r. 529–522 B.C.), the son and successor of Cyrus, who spent most of his rule trying to conquer Egypt for the Persians.

Cyrus (r. c. 559–530 B.C.): Founder of the Achaemenid Dynasty, Cyrus was the leader of the Persians, an Iranian people. Cyrus further expanded his empire from southern Iran to include Babylonia, Assyria, Syria-Palestine, and Asia Minor. In 538 B.C. he allowed the Jews to return to Jerusalem.

Darius I (r. 521–c. 486 B.C.): Darius was a Persian nobleman who took the throne of Persia in a palace coup after the death of Cambyses. He recorded a detailed description of his rise to the throne on a rock-cut inscription at Mt. Behistun/Besitun. In 490 B.C., Darius ordered the first invasion of Greece by the Persians.

Darius III (r. 336–331 B.C.): The last Persian King, defeated by Alexander in 331 at Guagamela.

Eannatum (r. c. 2450–2425 B.C.): A king of Lagash near the end of the war between the cities of Umma and Lagash.

Enheduanna: Daughter of Sargon I of Akkad (r. c. 2334–2279 B.C.) who was made the high priestess of Nanna at Ur. This act allowed her father to solidify his control over north and south Mesopotamia.

In her position as priestess, she was the author of several hymns to the goddess and is the first named author in history.

Esarhaddon (r. 680–669 B.C.): Younger son and successor of Sennacherib, who attacked Babylon in retribution for rebellion. Esarhaddon had been a governor of Babylonia, and this may have encouraged him to begin rebuilding the city as soon as he took the throne. His rule was known for its internal stability.

Gudea (r. c. 2100 B.C.): Ruler of the city-state of Lagash after the fall of the Akkadian dynasty. Gudea is well known from many portraits that show him as a pious ruler.

Hammurabi (r. 1792–1750 B.C.): Ruler of Babylon who expanded his territory to control all of northern and southern Mesopotamia and northern Syria after he destroyed the city of Mari. Hammurabi is credited with creating the longest surviving law code.

Herodotus (b. c. 484, d. between 430–420 B.C.): Greek historian known as the "father of history," he described Persian customs, history, and the two invasions of Darius and Xerxes into Greece.

Ibbi-Sin (r. c. 2028–2004 B.C.): Last king of the Ur III dynasty.

Nabonidus (r. c. 555–539 B.C.): Ruler who alienated Babylonia after he moved the capital to a desert oasis in the Arabian desert, perhaps because he wished to promote the worship of the moon god Sin.

Nabopolassar (r. 626–605 B.C.): A local ruler of Babylonia, Nabopolassar took the throne at a time when the Assyrian Empire was weak. He united all of Babylonia under his rule, allied with the Elamites, and attacked and destroyed the Assyrian capital at Nineveh in 612 B.C.

Naram-Sin (r. c. 2254–2218 B.C.): Grandson of the Akkadian ruler Sargon, Naram-Sin was the first ruler to represent himself as a god and to deify himself. This may have led to many negative depictions of Naram-Sin in later generations.

Nebuchadnezzar (r. c. 604–562 B.C.): Babylonian ruler who succeeded his father, Nabopolassar. He destroyed Jerusalem in 587 B.C., burning the temple of Solomon and deporting most of the population of Israel to Babylonia. Nebuchadnezzar also sponsored many building projects in Babylon; this was the city that was best known to Greek visitors, who described its wonders. Also called Nebuchadrezzar III.

Pu-Abi (r. c. 2500 B.C.): Sumerian queen whose jewelry was found in the Royal Cemetery at Ur.

Rim-Sin (r. 1822–1763 B.C.): Ruler of Larsa who controlled much of southern Mesopotamia in the early part of Hammurabi's rule. Rim-Sin ruled longer than any other king in Mesopotamia.

Sammuramat (r. c. 811–806 B.C.): Queen mother who was regent with her son Adad-Nirari III; this Assyrian queen may have been the inspiration for the legend of Semiramis. Assyrian sources give her name but no other details about her life or rule.

Sargon of Akkad (r. c. 2334–2279 B.C.): Founder of the Akkadian Dynasty.

Sargon II (r. c. 721–705 B.C.): Assyrian ruler who, like his Akkadian predecessor, claimed by his name that he was the "legitimate king." Sargon was successful in quelling rebellions in the west and in Babylonia. Sargon founded a new Assyrian capital at Dur-Sharru-ken, Fort Sargon, but it was abandoned after his death.

Sennacherib (r. c. 704/705–681 B.C.): The son and successor of Sargon II, Sennacherib was known for his siege and destruction of Babylon in 689 B.C. This unusual attack by an Assyrian ruler on an important cultural capital was denounced by Babylonian sources.

Shalmaneser III (r. c. 858–824 B.C.): Assyrian ruler who defeated a coalition of western rulers, Egyptian, Israelite, and other rulers from Syria and Palestine, at Qarqar in 853 B.C. Continued the building project at Nimrud begun by his father, Ashurnasirpal II.

Shamshi-Adad (r. c. 1808–1776 B.C.): Ruler who took control of Ashur and was the first king to expand the heartland of Ashur into a small kingdom. Shamshi-Adad installed his son, Yasmah-Adad, on the throne of Mari but was frustrated by his son's undisciplined behavior.

Shulgi (r. c. 2094–2047 B.C.): Ruler of Ur during the Ur III period, which is especially well documented. Shulgi instituted several administrative reforms and was the subject of many hymns celebrating his reign.

Tiglath-Pileser III (r. c. 744–727 B.C.): King of Assyria during the second and most extensive phase of the Assyrian Empire.

Ur-Nammu (r. c. 2112–2094 B.C.): First of the five kings of the Ur III dynasty.

Xerxes (r. 486–465 B.C.): Persian king who succeeded his father, Darius I, and invaded Greece in 480 B.C. The Greek historian Herodotus wrote a memorable description of this tyrannical ruler, who commanded a vast army but was defeated by the Greeks. His later years are not well known.

Zimri-Lim (r. c. 1776–1761 B.C.): Ruler of the city of Mari on the northern Euphrates during the reign of Hammurabi. His large and well-appointed palace was destroyed by Hammurabi after several years of alliance with the Babylonian king.

Bibliography

Essential Reading:

Aruz, Joan, ed. *Art of the First Cities: The Third Millennium B.C. from the Mediterranean to the Indus*. New York: Metropolitan Museum of Art, 2003. Museum catalog of art from all of the major civilizations of the 3rd millennium. Historical summaries and detailed entries. Beautifully illustrated.

Bahn, Paul C. *Archaeology: A Very Short Introduction*. Oxford: Oxford University Press, 1996. A survey of archaeological methods and techniques. Also includes a discussion of the research goals of archaeologists.

Black, Jeremy, and Anthony Green. *Gods, Demons and Symbols of Ancient Mesopotamia*. London: British Museum Press, 1992. A standard dictionary for Mesopotamian religion. Short but detailed entries; good bibliography.

Bogdanos, Matthew, and William Patrick. *Thieves of Baghdad*. London: Bloomsbury, 2005. Account of the attempt to recover the artifacts looted from the Iraq Museum by the American representative to the museum.

Bottéro, Jean. *Mesopotamia: Writing, Reasoning, and the Gods*. Zainab Bahrani and Marc Van De Mieroop, trans. Chicago: University of Chicago Press, 1995. Topics include religion, science, and the development of writing in Mesopotamia and Elam.

———. *The Oldest Cuisine in the World: Cooking in Mesopotamia*. Teresa Lavender Fagan, trans. Chicago: University of Chicago Press, 2004. Surveys the written evidence for food, cooking, beer and wine, and some feasting occasions.

Briant, Pierre. *From Cyrus to Alexander: A History of the Persian Empire*. Winona Lake: Eisenbrauns, 2002. Detailed coverage of the rise and fall of the Achaemenid Empire.

Chavalas, Mark W., ed. *The Ancient Near East: Historical Sources in Translation*. Oxford: Blackwell Publishing, 2006. Primary sources for Near Eastern history from c. 2700 B.C. to the Hellenistic period (c. 250 B.C.).

Collon, Dominique. *Ancient Near Eastern Art*. London: British Museum Press, 1995. One of the standard handbooks of Near Eastern monuments and archaeology, focused on the collection in the British Museum.

Cunningham, Graham, Jeremy Black, Eleanor Robson, and Gabor Zolyomi, eds. *The Literature of Ancient Sumer*. Oxford: Oxford University Press, 2006. Translation of several genres of Sumerian literature and historical documents.

Curtis, John, and N. Tallis, eds. *Forgotten Empire: The World of Ancient Persia*. Berkeley: University of California Press, 2005. Exhibit catalog that illustrates the wealth and luxury of the Persians. Articles also explore burial customs, Persian religion, and the economy.

Dalley, Stephanie. *Mari and Karana: Two Old Babylonian Cities*. Piscataway, NJ: Gorgias Press, 2002. Overview of the archaeological and written evidence that survives from two contemporary cities of the 18th and 19th centuries B.C. Thematic sections on women, warfare, and more.

———. .*Myths from Mesopotamia: Creation, the Flood, Gilgamesh and Others*. Oxford: Oxford University Press, 1989. Clear translations of the major Mesopotamian myths in one volume; useful for comparing mythical themes and styles.

Foster, Benjamin R. *The Epic of Gilgamesh: A New Translation, Analogues, Criticism*. New York and London: W.W. Norton, 2001. Translation with illustration of relevant images, additional stories that involve Gilgamesh, and scholarly analyses of different aspects of the myth.

———. *From Distant Days: Myths, Tales and Poetry of Ancient Mesopotamia*. Baltimore: Johns Hopkins University Press, 1995. A sampling of Sumerian and Akkadian literature. This book provides an excellent introduction to the common themes in surviving mythical, historical, proverbial, and magical texts.

Green, Peter C. *Alexander of Macedon, 356–323 B.C.: A Historical Biography*. Berkeley: University of California Press, 1992. Detailed history of the career of Alexander the Great and his encounters with the Persians.

Herodotus. *The Histories*. Aubrey de Selincourt, trans. New York: Penguin USA, 2003. Greek historian of the 5th century B.C. who describes the culture and history of the Persian Empire, with a focus on the two invasions of Greece.

Kuhrt, Amélie. *The Ancient Near East, c. 3000–330 BC*. London and New York: Routledge, 1997. A two-volume detailed history of the

Near East and Egypt. This work centers on the political history of the era. Excellent bibliography.

Maier, John, ed. *Gilgamesh: A Reader*. Wauconda, IL: Bolchazy-Carducci, 1997. Large collection of scholarly articles on many topics and approaches to the epic. Very useful bibliography.

Matthews, Roger. *The Archaeology of Mesopotamia: Theory and Approaches*. London and New York: Routledge, 2003. Short but detailed history of the archaeological methods used in Mesopotamia, as well as the various theoretical approaches scholars apply.

Moran, William L. *The Amarna Letters*. Baltimore: John Hopkins University Press, 2002. English translation of the Amarna letters; historical overview and explanatory notes are included.

Plutarch, *The Life of Alexander the Great*. Translated by Ian Scott-Kilvert. London: Penguin Books, 1973. One of the first attempts to memorialize the legendary king.

Polk, Milbry, and Angela M. H. Shuster, eds. *Looting of the Baghdad Museum: The Lost Legacy of Ancient Mesopotamia*. New York: H.A. Abrams, 2005. Illustrated overview of Mesopotamian history that employs the objects looted, some of which have been recovered, at the Iraq Museum.

Pollock, Susan. *Ancient Mesopotamia: The Eden That Never Was*. Cambridge: Cambridge University Press, 1999. Survey of early Mesopotamia, discussed topically and with special reference to the archaeological theories applied to material culture.

Postgate, J. Nicholas. *Early Mesopotamia: Society and Economy at the Dawn of History*. London and New York: Routledge, 1992. Topical study of the early history of Mesopotamia. Especially good for analysis of social institutions and interpretation of the evidence for this early period.

Roaf, Michael. *Cultural Atlas of Mesopotamia and the Ancient Near East*. New York: Facts on File, 1990. Clear, thoroughly illustrated textbook of the history and art of Mesopotamia. Excellent maps and brief descriptions of the major sites included in a historical overview of the region.

Roth, Martha T. *Law Collections from Mesopotamia and Asia Minor*. 2nd ed. Atlanta: Society of Biblical Literature, 1997. Recent translations of all the surviving law codes; a brief historical commentary for each collection.

Roux, Georges. *Ancient Iraq*. 3rd ed. New York: Penguin USA, 1993. History of Mesopotamia from the rise of the city through the Persian Empire. Somewhat out of date, but it remains an excellent analysis of all aspects of Mesopotamian life and culture.

Sasson, Jack, ed. *Civilizations of the Ancient Near East*. Peabody, MA: Hendrickson Publishers, 2001 (reprint). Thorough study of the history, culture, and archaeology of Egypt and the Near East, including Anatolia. Succinct articles written by experts in the field; bibliographical section at the end of each section for further study.

Tetlow, Elizabeth M. *Women, Crime and Punishment in Ancient Law and Society: Mesopotamia*. London: Continuum Publishing Group, 2005. Study of Mesopotamian women through the laws of the different cultures covered in the course.

Van De Mieroop, Marc. *The Ancient Mesopotamian City*. Oxford: Oxford University Press, 1997. Van De Mieroop draws on evidence from multiple sites and historical eras to provide a full and interesting study of life in Mesopotamian cities.

———. *A History of the Ancient Near East, ca. 3000–323 BC*. Second Edition. Oxford: Blackwell, 2006. Textbook that sets out the history and scholarly debates of the Near East (Egypt not included).

———. *Cuneiform Texts and the Writing of History*. London and New York: Routledge, 1999. Description of the challenges of interpreting cuneiform texts; clearly written.

———. *King Hammurabi of Babylon*. London: Blackwell, 2006. Biography of the king best known for his law codes; this history places the ruler within the political and cultural framework of the era.

Zettler, Richard, and Lee Horne, eds. *Treasures from the Royal Tombs at Ur*. Philadelphia: University of Pennsylvania Press, 1998. Catalog of the objects discovered in the Royal Cemetery at Ur and a reevaluation of the excavation and interpretation of the site.

Supplementary Reading:

Adkins, Lesley. *Empires of the Plain: Henry Rawlinson and the Lost Languages of Babylon*. New York: Thomas Dunne Books, 2003. A detailed account of the early expeditions in Mesopotamia with special reference to the decipherment of cuneiform.

Allen, Lindsay. *The Persian Empire*. Chicago: University of Chicago Press, 2005. Survey of the history and culture of the Persian Empire;

also includes a discussion of the legacy of the Persians to the 20th century. Very well illustrated.

Boardman, John. *Persia and the West. An Archaeological Investigation of the Genesis of Achaemenid Art.* London: Thames & Hudson, 2000. Analysis of Persian art, the blending of different artistic styles, and Persian influence on Western art.

Cawkwell, George. *The Greek Wars: The Failure of Persia.* Oxford: Oxford University Press, 2005. Detailed analysis of the strategic, military, and diplomatic history of the Persian invasions of Greece.

Christie, Agatha. *Murder in Mesopotamia.* New York: Penguin USA, 1987. Mystery focused on Mesopotamia written by the wife of one of the leading British archaeologists, Max Mallowan, who excavated at Nineveh.

Cohen, Raymond, and Raymond Westbrooks, eds. *Amarna Diplomacy: The Beginnings of International Relations.* Baltimore: Johns Hopkins University Press, 2002. International relations scholars examine the Amarna letters to explore these early attempts at diplomacy.

Heimpel, Wolfgang. *Letters to the King of Mari.* Winona Lake, IL: Einsenbrauns, 2003. Collection of translated letters found at Mari in the palace destroyed by Hammurabi; includes a historical introduction and commentary.

Kampen, Natalie B., and Bettina Bergmann, eds. *Sexuality in Ancient Art.* Cambridge: Cambridge University Press, 1996. See the article by Irene J. Winter on the stele of Naram-Sin and the significance of his self-divinization.

Nissen, Hans J. *The Early History of the Ancient Near East: 9000–2000 BC.* Chicago: University of Chicago Press, 1988. A close study of the archaeological evidence and theories of interpretation for the rise of urbanization.

Oates, Joan. *Babylon.* 2nd ed. London: Thames & Hudson, 1986. History of the city and culture of Babylon, with special attention to the city and the archaeology of the site.

———. *Nimrud: An Assyrian Imperial City Revealed.* London: British School of Archaeology in Iraq, 2001. Close study of the excavations at Nimrud, with detailed descriptions and illustrations of the palace and finds there.

Oppenheim, A. Leo. *Ancient Mesopotamia*. 2nd ed. Chicago: University of Chicago Press, 1977. Somewhat out of date in its historical interpretations but an interesting study of the social institutions of Mesopotamia.

Pollock, Susan, and Reinhard Bernbeck, eds. *Archaeologies of the Middle East: Critical Perspectives*. Oxford: Blackwell Publishing, 2005. Scholarly articles addressing specific periods, theoretical approaches, and the historiography of the Middle East.

Snell, Daniel C. *Life in the Ancient Near East*. New Haven: Yale University Press, 1997. Chronological history of the Near East, with emphasis on economic history.

———, ed. *A Companion to the Ancient Near East*. London: Blackwell Press, 2005. A collection of articles on such topics as the changing environment, cities, laws, and the legacy of Mesopotamia.

Stone, Elizabeth C., and Paul Zimansky. "Mashkan-shapir and the Anatomy of an Old Babylonian City." *Biblical Archaeologist* 55 (1993). Discussion of Mashkan-shapir, one of the most prominent cities in Mesopotamia.

———, "Mesopotamian Cities and Countryside," in Daniel C. Snell, ed. *A Companion to the Ancient Near East*. Malden: Blackwell Press, 2005. A comprehensive overview of Near Eastern civilization from the Bronze Age to the campaigns of Alexander the Great.

Walker, C. B. F. *Cuneiform*. London: British Museum Press, 1987. Brief overview of the development of cuneiform and the evidence found in cuneiform texts.

Woolley, Sir Leonard. *Digging up the Past*. New York: Greenwood Press Reprint, 1978. Lively description of the exciting discoveries at the Royal Cemetery of Ur by one of the leading British archaeologists active in Iraq.